T0315371

Protecting Critical Infrastructures Against Cyber-Attack

Stephen J. Lukasik, Seymour E. Goodman and David W. Longhurst

Routledge
Taylor & Francis Group

LONDON AND NEW YORK

ADELPHI PAPER 359

© The International Institute for Strategic Studies 2003

First published August 2003 by **Oxford University Press** for
The International Institute for Strategic Studies

Published 2015 by Routledge
4 Park Square, Milton Park, Abingdon, Oxon OX14 4RN
711 Third Avenue, New York, NY 10017

Routledge is an imprint of the Taylor & Francis Group, an informa business

for The International Institute for Strategic Studies
Arundel House, 13–15 Arundel Street, Temple Place, London WC2R 3DX, UK
www.iiss.org

Director John Chipman
Editor Tim Huxley
Copy Editor Matthew Foley
Production Simon Nevitt

British Library Cataloguing in Publication Data
Data available

Library of Congress Cataloguing in Publication Data

ISBN 13: 978-0-19-853016-9 (pbk)
ISSN 0567-932X

Contents

Glossary

CESG	Communication-Electronics Security Group
CMU	Carnegie Mellon University
DTI	Department of Trade and Industry
GCHQ	Government Communications Headquarters
FOC	Full Operational Capability
IAAC	Information Assurance Advisory Council
IOC	Initial Operational Capability
IPO	Initial Public Offering
ISAC	Information Sharing and Analysis Center
LDC	Less-developed country
MoD	Ministry of Defence
NISCC	National Infrastructure Security Co-ordination Centre
PDD-63	Presidential Decision Directive 63
PKI	Public Key Infrastructure

Introduction

National infrastructures such as the electricity grid, telecommunications system and transport network provide services that we use daily, supporting the physical functioning of society. These services are based on capital-intensive facilities for which standby capacity is frequently difficult and expensive. Both for operational efficiency and to enable back-up capabilities, these facilities are increasingly reliant on interconnected computer systems. System operators are in turn becoming dependent on complex software that is at best imperfectly understood, and whose failures are difficult to predict. Components fail, accidents occur and sabotage can happen. If parts of the national infrastructure malfunction, this can have a significant impact on the physical and economic well-being of a country and its people.

Three factors compound the problem. First, while the probability of random events can be calculated with a degree of reliability, malicious acts are not random: they are the result of planning and analysis to identify worst possible outcomes.

Second, the tendency to integrate separate local parts of the infrastructure for greater efficiency means that a country's vulnerability to both physical and cyber-attack increases with the number of potential access points. By exploiting flaws in the software, vulnerabilities in the architecture or human imperfection, attackers can, in principle, cause large-scale damage with relatively little effort. While integration can make a system more robust by introducing redundancy, experience suggests that the net impact of increasing complexity is to increase, rather than decrease, vulnerability to failure and attack.

Third, industrial restructuring, the pressure to reduce 'less productive' actions that increase costs, the specialisation of functions, outsourcing and regulatory pressures further complicate the protection of infrastructures. Their combined effect is to introduce organisational interfaces at which errors can occur, where responsibility is diffuse, where open access is mandated, and hence where intruders can enter.

Some governments have been aware of these issues, and have postulated the threats to their national security. To address these concerns, each country is likely to seek a strategy that reflects its assessment of both the seriousness of the threat that infrastructure disruption poses, and the appropriate counteractions to reduce the risk to acceptable levels.

Chapter 1 reviews the current vulnerability of infrastructure systems to attack. Chapter 2 presents a taxonomy of the strategic defence options open to national governments. Chapter 3 examines public and private roles in implementing the various strategic options. Chapter 4 provides a framework for selecting from these options. In Chapter 5, this generic treatment of the problem is applied to the current situation in the US and the UK. Chapter 6 compares strategies and actions suggested by the framework with programmes directed at critical infrastructure protection in the US and the UK. Chapter 7 addresses the broader applicability of the strategic framework. States can be viewed in terms of the degree to which their national infrastructures are vulnerable to attack. As part of this discussion, Sweden is examined in some detail, providing further insight into the applicability of the framework presented here. The paper concludes that aside from specific measures each nation may undertake on its own behalf, there is a need for global standards and global cooperation to protect the infrastructures on which all nations depend.

Chapter 1

The Vulnerabilities of National Infrastructures

Infrastructure Interdependencies

The potential vulnerability of a single integrated infrastructure system is compounded by the interdependence that arises between infrastructures. This is because the provision of service by one system generally depends on services from other infrastructures. Identifying such interdependence was an important part of the preparation for the year 2000 (Y2K) rollover, when managers were in danger of being caught out by failures in systems on which they were dependent.

One particularly revealing study for the Cabinet Office in the UK analysed 11 infrastructures: fuel, utilities, transport, finance, the supply of food and goods, communication, emergency services, social services, justice, health services and weather forecasting.[2] Each was then broken down into 59 'processes', each of which was examined to identify the generic actions required for their operation. It was thus possible to identify for each process which other processes it depended upon.

This analysis identified the most critical processes on which the greatest number of others depends. Table 1 (see over) shows the most important ones. The table shows the number of critical dependencies (C); the number of non-critical dependencies (N); and the sum of both (T). There are four processes in the most critical category, and eight in the next tier of criticality. Not surprisingly, telecommunications and electric power are the most critical processes, on which virtually all the others depend. The supply of transport fuel and the road infrastructure rank third and fourth, since most material goods move from producer

Table 1 The Most Critical Infrastructure Processes

Infrastructure Process	C (Critical)	N (Non-Critical)	T (Total)
Telecommunications	49	9	58
Electricity	56	1	57
Fuel supplies for transport	45	4	49
Road infrastructure	43	6	49
Clean water	26	3	29
Fund transfers	17	3	20
Postal service	14	3	17
Gas supplies	13	3	16
Sanitation and waste disposal	11	4	15
Fire and rescue service	11	2	13
Weather information	9	10	19
Rail transport	8	11	19

to consumer by road. The next tier includes the supply of water and gas, the movement of funds and the emergency services. These central systems are the ones a state-supported attacker is most likely to target.

Infrastructure failures and infrastructure attacks

The concerns over infrastructure vulnerability are to a large extent based on the extrapolation of trends and plausibility arguments. What are the threats that would justify a major national defence effort? First, both strategic and theatre infrastructure systems have always been targets for military attack. Tying the parts of these infrastructures together through the use of information technology opens the possibility of new ways to attack the same targets, and hence new requirements for civil and military defence.

Second, infrastructure systems fail due to the malfunction of their parts and the stress of the natural environment. The interconnection of systems increases the likelihood that failure at one location will affect ever-larger service areas.

Third, there is a growing body of experience relating specifically to infrastructure attacks by cyber-techniques, or where cyber-related vulnerabilities have played an important part. Two cases are noteworthy. On 7 February 2000, two websites were subjected to a distributed denial of service attack. To mount such an attack, the attacker secures access to a number of unprotected computers and instructs them to send a large number of messages to the target website, either requesting information and hence saturating the target's input capacity, or transmitting invalid information that causes the target site to crash. The first attack was on Yahoo at 1:10pm Eastern Standard Time (EST), and shut the site down for five hours.[3] Yahoo is visited by 8.7 million (m) users per day, and is an important part of the Internet because it serves as a portal to locate other sites or information. At 2pm on the same day, Buy.com was attacked and closed down for six hours. This e-commerce sales site is visited by 122,000 users per day. On 8 February Amazon.com, a retail sales site visited by 892,000 users daily, was closed for 3.75 hours; the CNN news site, with 642,000 users a day, was closed for 3.5 hours; and the eBay auction site, with 1.68m users, was closed for five hours. This pattern was repeated on 9 February. The E*Trade brokerage site, with 183,000 users daily, was closed for 2.75 hours and ZDNet (734,000 users) closed for 3.25 hours.[4]

The cost of these attacks is difficult to ascertain.[5] Subsequent estimates have put the cost at hundreds of millions of dollars, but such numbers are quite soft.[6] When dealing with insurers, or to impress policymakers, there is an incentive to inflate the figures, and when dealing with shareholders and regulators, there is an incentive to deflate them.

Although not primarily cyber-related, protests against rising fuel prices in the UK in September 2000 illustrate the possible effects of an attack on a national infrastructure. On 7 September 2000, protesters blockaded the British Shell refinery at Stanlow. By 10 September, there were blockades at 11 refineries and fuel depots. The rate of departure of fuel tankers from a typical refinery was reduced from one every three minutes to one every hour, for emergency services only. By 12 September, fuel supplies were reduced to zero or near zero at 320 of 960 Texaco filling stations, 350 of 1,600 Esso stations and 600 of 1,500 BP stations; the situation was similar for other chains. By the morning of 13 September, petrol companies estimated that 90% of their stations would run out of fuel.[7]

These protests illustrate the effectiveness of an attack on an infrastructure on which a large number of other systems depends, and provides support for the infrastructure interdependency analysis shown in Table 1.[8] Panic buying of bread and milk ensued. Supermarket chain Safeway instituted rationing and Asda said it could not guarantee supplies beyond 16 September. The Royal Mail warned that it had supplies for only one more day of deliveries in some areas. Banks warned that they were running out of cash. The British Airports Authority advised airlines to refuel at Heathrow or Gatwick because these airports were served by private pipelines. Bus operators claimed that they had fuel to provide for 75% of normal service until 15 September. Train operators reported that they had supplies only until 15 September. The Confederation of British Industry stated that production lines would start shutting down because of loss of raw materials, and that there was no storage available for unshipped inventory.[9]

The protesters withdrew their blockades on 14 September when it became apparent that public opinion was turning against them.[10] The British Institute of Directors said UK companies faced a loss of $1.4 billion; the hotel industry, manufacturing and transport were especially badly hit. The London Chamber of Commerce estimated that the fuel crisis was costing £250m per day, and that 10% of the UK's daily output of £2.5bn was being lost. The loss to businesses in London was £50m per day.

This attack was made more effective through the widespread use of information technology. Mobile phones allowed the rapid deployment of protesters through organised call networks. Information technology also allowed the need-related delivery of raw materials and goods, resulting in smaller inventories less capable of supporting normal operations over extended periods of disruption.

These examples do not, by themselves, constitute a call to action. The point is simply that infrastructure attacks are feasible, costly to the target country, and, if their effects persist long enough, can weaken national economies and endanger lives.[11] The interdependency analysis in Table 1 can aid defenders in allocating resources and establishing priorities. By the same token, attackers can use it in formulating effective campaign strategies.

Models for information attacks on infrastructure

For the purpose of this discussion, attackers can be of two types. They may be non-state actors whose purposes are criminal and who are subject to the jurisdiction of one or more sovereign states. Their attacks constitute crimes against individuals and property. Terrorists constitute a more serious set of non-state actors and are of concern both to law enforcement agencies and national security agencies.

The second type of attacker is a sovereign state waging information warfare. This attacker's targets are other sovereign states, although specific targets may be identical to those of non-state attackers. Defence against these attackers is a responsibility of both external and internal security and intelligence agencies, acting in concert.

The hacker currently garners the greatest amount of public attention. Hackers may not seek to cause damage, but their actions are nevertheless disruptive. The earliest examples of such behaviour were 'phone phreaks' whose intentions were both to satisfy their intellectual curiosity and impress their peers, as well as to defraud communications carriers. The majority of attacks on computer systems, which number in the thousands each year, are by hackers.[12] Most result in little infrastructure damage, although some accidental damage has been recorded.[13] Such attackers are not of primary interest here, but they do serve the useful purpose of preventing complacency about the security of information systems and the vulnerability of countries that, of necessity, depend on them. If an enthusiastic amateur can penetrate major systems designed and operated by professionals, serious coordinated attacks against a country cannot be safely ignored.

Research by Raymond Parks and others at the Sandia National Laboratory in the US shows how an attacker might operate.[14] An attacker will use a variety of open-source data to select targets, and will use widely available means of attack and information about a system's vulnerabilities to identify possible approaches to them.[15] This intelligence collection and detailed preparation will consume the bulk of the attacker's time. At various times during this period, the attacker will undertake live system testing, system discovery and attack practice. The final attack will consume the least amount of the attacker's time.

The attacker must remain undetected throughout this preparatory period. Early discovery of an attacker or attack plan can be crucial, so that the detection of an attacker's probes and their identification as attack precursors is an important element of defence. Such information can reveal the intended targets and the path to them.

Depending on the nature of the target and the attacker's objectives, damage can occur rapidly, as in denial of service or triggered 'Trojan Horse' attacks. The impact of other attacks, such as viruses distributed by e-mail, grows more slowly. Attacks can be distributed over time if the attacker's plan is to reduce the effectiveness of a national system by changing the specific targets over a period of days, such as an extended series of attacks on separate emergency telephone systems.

Similarly, reconstitution can occur at various rates. A central system can be reconstituted by rebooting it and reverting to its pre-attack state using system backups, but this can be costly and some information will be lost. Other cases, such as the complete shutdown of an electricity distribution system, can require a substantial amount of time for black-start or, in the case of multiple points of physical damage, for the dispatching of repair personnel. Thus, onset times, attack duration and recovery time depend a great deal on the nature of the system attacked and on the ability of the attacker to maintain a continuous series of information 'sorties', in effect to conduct a cyber-campaign against an adversary state.

Much of this thinking is speculative since such cyber-warfare campaigns have so far only taken place in planned exercises. But the targeting concepts for information attacks are a translation of what has long been understood about the conduct of other forms of offensive military operations.

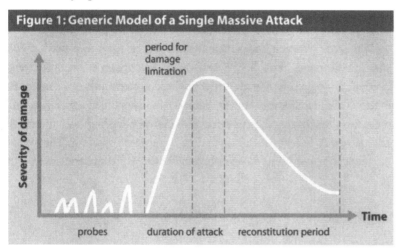

Figure 1: Generic Model of a Single Massive Attack

These time relationships are shown generically in Figure 1. An ability to limit damage during an attack will depend on the rate of onset of damage, the ability of the defender to sense the attack and to take remedial action, and the ability of the attacker to remain effective. Ample models of one-on-one military combat illustrate the fundamental concepts.

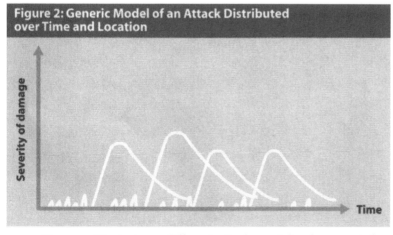

Figure 2: Generic Model of an Attack Distributed over Time and Location

Figure 2 illustrates a different attack model, where an infrastructure system is subjected to a series of attacks distributed over an extended period and directed at various parts of an interconnected national system. For example, an air transport system need not be attacked at all points. The performance of the system can be impaired over a long period if it is attacked one city at a time.

This kind of attack on a distributed infrastructure exploits its distributed, but integrated, nature by attacking its most vulnerable points over time. If the rate of attacks is sufficiently great compared to system reconstitution times, the system can be kept in a permanent state of damage. Thus in the case of air transport, if enough users become dismayed at the apparent risk, the system fails not due to its internal deficiencies but simply because the users find other ways to meet their needs and the system is reduced to handling only the most critical needs for which it is uniquely capable of meeting. The situation might be captured by the phrase 'death by a thousand cuts.'

Chapter 2

Strategic Defence Options

Faced with the possibility of serious disruption to their national infrastructures, governments can be expected to plan and implement prudent defensive actions. Public policies aimed at protecting infrastructures will, in the majority of countries, require a clear logic relating perceived states of vulnerability to the desired aim of those defensive policies.

Such logic will require each country to identify those infrastructures critical to its survival and to its social and economic well-being. Since defensive actions will imply costs of various sorts – which each country will seek to minimise – it will be important that defensive measures are not too burdensome. Governments need to have sufficient understanding of their national infrastructures, including their interdependencies, so that they can determine both the efficiency and the effectiveness of the proposed defence.

Absolute defence against attack has rarely been achieved. Each defensive measure generates a countermeasure by an attacker, driving the defender to adopt ever-stronger measures. This sequence of action and counteraction is common in adversarial relationships, and is most obvious and best understood in the interaction of opposing military forces. The concept of cost–exchange ratio may be useful in this case. Put simply, defenders should not expend large amounts of resources on measures that can be cheaply and easily defeated by an attacker; rather, defensive measures should be designed to require the attacker to spend inordinately greater resources to defeat them.

Figure 3 suggests that protecting infrastructure systems involves five related issues. First, it is necessary to attempt to deter potential attackers. Second, if attacked, the need is to thwart the attack

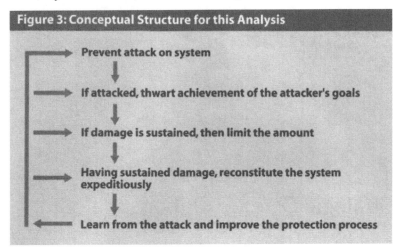

Figure 3: Conceptual Structure for this Analysis

Prevent attack on system

If attacked, thwart achievement of the attacker's goals

If damage is sustained, then limit the amount

Having sustained damage, reconstitute the system expeditiously

Learn from the attack and improve the protection process

and to prevent damage. Third, since success cannot be guaranteed in either preventing or thwarting an attack, the next best tactic is to limit the damage as far as possible. Fourth, having sustained some level of damage from an attack, the defender must reconstitute the pre-attack state of affairs. Finally, since both offence and defence are influenced by changing technology and incentives to attack, the defender must learn from failure, just as attackers will learn from theirs.[1]

There will be trade-offs between the various courses of action suggested by this conceptual structure. Preventing or thwarting attacks can be costly and may incur losses through reduced system performance. The greater the success in limiting damage, the less damage there is to be repaired. If limiting damage is difficult, it will be better to invest in assisting reconstitution. Damage limitation can be viewed on two time-scales. Plans can be made to limit the damage from a single attack, or to minimise losses from multiple attacks over time. There will be trade-offs here too, between the detailed and potentially costly scrutiny of individual transactions and the identification and punishment of attackers over the longer term, recognising that this means sustaining some damage.

Since an infrastructure system is typically under mixed public and private ownership, the various owners are likely to have different views about investing in protection. Private owners, faced with loss of revenue and loss of confidence by customers, regulators, investors and insurers, will seek to restore revenues and confidence in their stewardship. Governments will pursue policies that focus on longer-term aspects of protection, seeking to reduce cumulative losses, protect markets and maintain law and order. Professional and business associations representing infrastructure systems and their suppliers will hold both views in varying degrees: the long view for the benefit of their public customer base, while reflecting the individual financial and competitive concerns of their members over short term costs of protection.

Thus, public policy must represent a balance of short- and long-term approaches, as well as a balance between levels of investment in prevention, damage limitation and reconstitution.

Preventing an attack

There are at least three ways to prevent an attack. One is to deter the attacker by demonstrating the capability to inflict punishment. This implies that the attacker understands the risk of being identified and located, that the defender's resolve to punish is seen as credible and that the 'cost' of punishment favours the defender. A simple situation is when the attacker suffers a large 'front end' loss through discovery during the probe phase, and this discovery can be accomplished cheaply by the defender. When the cost of punishment is less for the defender than the loss that can be caused by the attacker, there will clearly be an incentive to develop ways of discovering attackers. But the more common situation is when the relatively high costs of legal prosecution are returned in reduced losses over the longer term.

Deterring criminal actions requires a certain level of international legal machinery, such as common definitions of what constitutes a crime, standards for the collection of forensic evidence and extradition agreements.[2] Deterring state attackers requires the defender to have a national policy that recognises information attacks as attacks under the UN Charter, justifying self-defence. A government and a private system owner will differ on how they view the costs of deterrence. National expenditures for a prompt capability to respond to attacks on the state include the correlation of intrusion events, the collection and dissemination of attack profiles and warnings and the costs of participation in international organisations and joint responses.

A second way to prevent an attack is by establishing cyber-attacks as unacceptable behaviour in the community of nations. This could be through formal arms control agreements, or through domestic laws and international agreements designed to protect privacy, property rights and other generally accepted areas of mutual interest. Again, the implication is that violators can be subjected to sanctions including social disapproval, civil or criminal penalties or the revocation of rights of access and use – a cyber equivalent of exile.

A third way to prevent an attack is to pre-empt the attacker. This implies a high level of national surveillance capability able to provide strategic warning. So stealthy are cyber-attacks, so widespread is the ability to plan and launch them, so inexpensive are the tools of attack and so lacking are the indicators that pre-emption would not yet appear to be a practical option. But should more responsible norms of behaviour in cyberspace be established, the detection and identification of abnormal behaviour may become easier.

For the most part, preventing cyber-attacks is the responsibility of sovereign states – for example, through law-enforcement agencies – which can threaten the use of various degrees of sovereign force and maintain a global surveillance capability to discover the intentions of potential adversaries.

Thwarting an attack

While prevention is largely based on governmental authority and responsibility, the detailed knowledge needed to thwart an attack rests primarily with the owner of the target. The least complicated case is where the system owner acts individually. The owner must not only be concerned with defence against outsiders, but must also recognise that not all authorised users of the system may have the owner's interests at heart.

There are many ways of defending systems against cyber-attack, and a certain number must be employed for the owner to demonstrate due diligence in protecting property rights. These will include requiring authorisation to enter, monitoring and recording the use of the system to detect unauthorised activities, periodic checking on the integrity of critical software and establishing and enforcing policies governing system security and responses to unexpected events. Owners can limit unauthorised activities by compartmentalising information within the system and maintaining need-to-know discipline. Owners have substantially more rights to monitor insider users whose access is covered by contractual terms governing employees and vendors.

There is considerably more potential for protecting systems when owners cooperate for their mutual benefit. In doing this there is a trade-off between the gain from the collective knowledge of a larger group and the potential loss due to the greater access to one's systems and information. If adequate controls govern cooperative defence, many types of information can be pooled: vulnerability, the rate and severity of attacks experienced by others, attack profiles and suspected attackers. Capabilities can also be pooled in security R&D, penetration testing, determining security standards and industry best practices and contributing to the establishment of educational and training curricula and the certification of professional security personnel.

A third approach is to build systems with a degree of intrusion-tolerance. These would aim to limit the effectiveness of single intruders through architectural approaches such as distributed control, multiple redundant systems with voting, the incorporation of air gaps and automated and manual monitoring of critical operations. Other approaches would include increasing the number of potential target points on which the attacker can expend resources, constructing virtual decoy facilities to distract attackers and internal compartmentalisation to contain damage. These have obvious parallels with defensive techniques ingrained in military planning, but are not typically part of the repertoire of the designers and administrators of computer systems.

Limiting damage during a successful attack

The central idea of this strategic objective is to limit damage in the attack period by constructing a 'battle management' system. The premised technical capability is the ability of the defender to audit a system's operation to be able to detect an attack and to take steps to limit the damage. The 'defender' can be at company, industry or national level.

Beyond being able to recognise that an attack is under way, damage limitation implies linking system operation centres to higher-level analysis centres for situation awareness and attack assessment. This also implies having pre-established response options at company, industry or national level.

Several kinds of response are possible. Adaptive defence allows the levels of defence to increase, such as calling for the re-authentication of all users or those currently undertaking critical functions or accessing critical information, putting critical transactions in 'quarantine' until they can be more thoroughly scrutinised, backing up system status, providing real-time warning to other systems and collecting larger amounts of forensic evidence.

Other responses might include active defence measures, such as tracing at the packet, message or session level, blocking traffic from or to an attacker's location and instituting legal actions to search and seize attacking computers. Such aggressive measures will generally be beyond the competence and jurisdiction of any but national authorities, and are likely to require broad determinations of national security. On the other hand, private entities acting either alone or cooperatively can undertake some of these responses, subject to their contractual agreements and regulatory limits on discriminatory behaviour.

Damage limitation can also include pre-planned redundancy and the establishment of a priority structure to dynamically reconfigure a system and reallocate load. This implies the capability to do system simulations in near real-time, as well as established and rehearsed response plans. Another possible approach may be to exploit local redundancy to support locally suitable responses (for example, handing off load to other sites in accordance with prior agreements to provide specified degrees of back-up).

Such near real-time responses, by their nature, reveal a capability to monitor, track, identify and take action against attackers. The decision to employ them requires weighing up the value of a response in each case against the long-term costs of revealing those capabilities and the nature and effectiveness of the adaptive responses.

Reconstituting after an attack

Short-term reconstitution is the set of first steps taken to meet the most urgent threats to life and property. They include assessing damage and implementing a recovery plan. Systems are restored from back-ups where possible, and residual resources may have to be rationed. Additional capacity may be generated as facilities that are idle or in maintenance are brought online. Online status reporting, online dispatching of emergency personnel and repair equipment, notifying users of possibly lost transactions, an ability to replan in near real-time and procedures for secure emergency communication will be required.

Long-term reconstitution of facilities and information may also be required, especially where physical damage has occurred. This will involve the identification and stockpiling of long-lead items (items that take a long time to replace because they are expensive or not stocked). Managing such risks will require industry-wide planning, to share surviving capacity, insure against loss and spread risk across insurers. The collection of loss data will enable both operators and insurers to manage risks most effectively. In the case of major loss, governments are likely to have an underwriting role.

All of these situations call for a healthy dose of worst-case planning. After-the-event analysis of system failures from natural events and lower-level attacks will aid in this process. Long-term reconstitution includes the last feedback loop in Figure 3, to use actual events to identify failure modes and solutions. It has to be a continuous process to address changing technical capabilities and circumstances.

Infrastructure owners bear the main responsibility for reconstitution, but government authorities and thus public assets are likely to be involved in the generation of emergency capacity and in underwriting recovery.

Improving the defender's performance

A current management paradigm asserts that organisations must learn from experience. However, events rarely unfold as expected, and even when they do social and technological change will probably diminish an organisation's effectiveness. There are therefore two responses. The first is to recognise the possibility of failure. The initial design of new systems or upgrades of existing systems should include a thorough analysis of potential flaws that an attacker could exploit. A defensive approach must be taken in system design, so that models of attackers and their strategies and tactics are established and tools for the collection of forensic data provided. An analogy is the design of a military combat system. While a system must meet its functional objectives, it is essential that, at the outset of the design process, consideration is given to defence against hostile action – not, as is often the case in commercial systems, at the end of the process, or even reactively. Information about the defence of the system should be concealed from potential attackers, and the system should be designed to give unsuccessful attackers as little information as possible on which to develop improved attacks. Finally, during the development process and after, deployment systems should be subject to independent penetration testing.

Post-attack analysis of intrusion attempts, whether successful or unsuccessful, is critical. While failure analysis is normal in some areas, such as a transport accident or building collapse, it is less common for information systems, where failures are more difficult to diagnose and forensic evidence harder to collect. The data that is gathered must be analysed, not only to assess damage, but also to thwart a recurrence of that attack and to address possible inadequacies in forensic data collection. While this may be shutting the stable door after the horse has bolted, successful attacks will be repeated, by the same attacker or others.

Table 2 Taxonomy of Strategic Defence Options and Tactical Objectives

Strategic Objective	Strategic Option	Tactical Objective
Prevent an attack on the system	Deter the attacker	Increase likelihood that the attack will be detected
		Identify and punish attacker
		Undertake to punish the sovereign nation to which the attacker is related, e.g. by citizenship, location, affiliation
	Establish standards of behaviour in cyberspace	Common understanding of unacceptable behaviour of users
		Identify and punish the attacker
		Agreement to abstain from attacks on critical systems
	Pre-empt attacker	Surveillance of potential attackers
Thwart attack on the system	Undertake individual terminal defence	Perimeter defence against outsiders
		Defence against insiders
		Document and control system interdependencies
	Undertake cooperative terminal defence	Combine independent defensive actions for greater overall effectiveness
		Spatial separation of links
	Build intrusion-tolerant systems	Limit the effectiveness of a single intruder through multiple independent controls
		Multiply attack points

Strategic Objective	Strategic Option	Tactical Objective
Limit damage to system	Audit system operation	Sense attack in near real-time
		Mount adaptive defence (local and/or global)
		Undertake active defence
	Pre-planned redundancy	Reallocate system load dynamically
Reconstitute system	Short-term reconstitution	Assess damage and implement recovery plan
		Restore system state from back-up records
		Ration residual resources and capacity
		Generate additional capacity
	Long-term reconstitution	Stockpile long-lead items in the event of physical damage
		Manage risk
Improve performance	Pre-attack preparation	Identify exploitable flaws
		Design systems defensively
		Protect system's defensive capabilities
	Post-attack learning	Analyse forensic data on attack
		Distribute results of post-attack analyses

Chapter 3

Implementing National Strategies: Actions and Actors

As a country considers its strategic options, it will want to understand the implications of their implementation. One question is technical feasibility, in terms of both current technology and future advances through R&D. A second consideration is the cost of implementation, especially weighed against the magnitude and imminence of the threat and the financial burden represented. Finally, the political implications must be considered, such as who bears responsibility; how far defence is mandatory; how far coordinated efforts in other countries will be required for success; and what balance is required between defensive and offensive capabilities. This chapter explores such implementation issues for the 12 strategic options identified in Table 2. Table 3 breaks down the capabilities that are required for each approach to preventing a cyber-attack, and suggests primary and secondary roles for the various participants.

The responsibility for deterring an attacker is shared between the system's owner and the national government. If the owner has installed effective intrusion-detection software, an intruder is more likely to concede defeat: their attack will be detected and they must assume that their actions will be recorded or thwarted. Secondary roles are played by national government and non-governmental organisations, which may assist the defender through, for example, information centres for collecting and disseminating attack warnings and validating detection software.

National governments' law-enforcement agencies will offer a more effective deterrent when an attacker has been identified and located. Criminal prosecution may be lengthy and costly but, if successful, will have some impact in deterring potential attackers by showing that the risks outweigh the gains. The more likely and the more severe the punishment, the greater the investment that the attacker must make and the longer it will take to prepare an attack, which in turn means that less capable attackers will be weeded out.

When the attacker is a sovereign state, an even wider set of national – political, conventional and cyber – responses is possible.

A long-term approach would be to reduce the lawless nature of cyberspace. This could be accomplished in a variety of ways: by instilling greater ethical sensitivity in new users of information systems; making clear that cyberspace is private, except those areas openly designated as public; defining the bounds of acceptable behaviour by law; and writing and enforcing contractual conditions on commercial transactions.

Sovereign states could agree not to undertake cyber-attacks on national infrastructures (a form of arms control). Such agreements, if they were to carry any weight, would need to be supported by verification capabilities to ensure that attacks can be detected and their source clearly identified.

Agreements on paper and standards of behaviour that are supported by the majority of 'netizens' will not influence criminals, terrorists or rogue states. However, the task of the defender will be aided immeasurably by the elimination of large numbers of casual assaults. Cyberspace is open to all, but if its environment is debased its utility will be severely reduced. The same holds for enhancing the quality and safety of the environment.

Responsibility is shared, with system owners having primary responsibility for informing and disciplining their users, and the national government playing the same role with respect to higher-level threats.

If cyberspace could be monitored, it might be possible to spot preparations for an attack and make a pre-emptive strike. This idea is borrowed from conventional military thinking, where preparations can be detected and action taken. The current state of cyber-intelligence and early warning makes such a response merely a theoretical possibility, but such capabilities could one day stabilise relations between states. This role would clearly fall to a national government, since the scope for private acts of pre-emption is limited.

Table 3 Preventing Cyber-Attacks: Capabilities and Roles

Strategic Option	Tactical Objective	Required Capabilities	Primary Role	Secondary Role
Deter attacker	Increase likelihood that attack will be detected	Detect attack	O/O	G or NGO
	Identify and punish attacker	Identify attacker	G and O/O	NGO
		Locate attacker	O/O	G or NGO
		Organisation response policies	O/O	G or NGO
		Legal jurisdiction and/or mutual assistance agreements among nations involved	G	
		Punishment guidelines	G	
	Identify and punish the sovereign nation responsible for the attack	National response policies	G	
Establish standards of behaviour	Common understanding of unacceptable behaviour of users	Instruction in ethical standards	O/O	NGO or G
		Contractual agreements with service providers	O/O	NGO or G
		Product specifications	O/O	NGO or G

(Continued on next page)

Strategic Option	Tactical Objective	Required Capabilities	Primary Role	Secondary Role
	Identify and punish attacker (see previous)	Define acceptable standards in law	see above	see above
	Agreement to abstain from attacks on critical national systems	Verification through the detection of attacks and the location of attackers	G	
Pre-empt attacker	Surveillance of potential attackers	Intelligence collection against potential attackers	G	
		Attack indicators	G	O/O
		National assessment capability	G	
		Response options: diplomatic, conventional military and cyber-capabilities	G	
		Identify attackers	O/O	G or NGO
		Collection of credible and releasable information for justification of actions	G	O/O
		Information sharing among allies	G	O/O

Note: The roles in the last two columns are abbreviated as follows:

O/O = Owner/Operator (can be either a private or a public entity)

G = National government

NGO = Non-governmental organisation(s)

Table 4 Thwarting Cyber-Attacks: Capabilities and Roles

Strategic Option	Tactical Objective	Required Capabilities	Primary Role	Secondary Role
Individual terminal defence	Perimeter defence against outsiders	Authentication of user as a condition for entry	O/O	
		Monitor and record information on incoming traffic	O/O	
		Compare incoming traffic with attack profiles	O/O	G or NGO
		Protected logs of audit data for post-attack analysis	O/O	
		Establish response policies and procedures	O/O	
		Penetration testing, reporting of results, implementation of fixes, auditing of effectiveness	O/O	G and NGO
	Defend against insiders	Monitor internal traffic (externals + content) in real-time and log for off-line analysis	O/O	
		Compartmentalisation and need-to-know	O/O	
		Vetting employees	O/O	G
		Establish response policies and procedures	O/O	

(Continued on next page)

Strategic Option	Tactical Objective	Required Capabilities	Primary Role	Secondary Role
Cooperative terminal defence	Document and control system interdependencies	A posteriori failure analysis	O/O	G
	Combine independent defensive actions for greater overall effectiveness	Pool vulnerability information	O/O	G
		Pool information on rate and severity of attacks	O/O	G
		Undertake cooperative R&D (e.g., testbed facilities, joint testing)	O/O	G
		Pool penetration test capability and its accreditation	O/O	G and NGO
		Establish industry best practices	O/O	G and NGO
		Participate in security standards efforts	O/O	G and NGO
		Cooperative investigation of system failures	O/O	G and NGO
		Contribute to the establishment of educational processes, curricula and professional certification	O/O	G and NGO
		Establish consumer cooperatives and vendor user groups	O/O	NGO

Strategic Option	Tactical Objective	Required Capabilities	Primary Role	Secondary Role
		Pool information on suspected attackers and attack modes	O/O	G
	Spatial separation of links	Attach geographical coordinates to routes and terminations	O/O	G
Build intrusion-tolerant systems	Limit single intruder effectiveness through multiple independent controls	Automated and manual monitoring of critical actions	O/O	
		Distributed control	O/O	
		Air gaps	O/O	
		Redundant independent subsystems with voting	O/O	
	Multiple attacks points	Decentralise system resources	O/O	
		Compartmentalisation and internal firewalls	O/O	
		Decoy systems	O/O	
		Honey pots and booby traps	O/O	

Note: The roles in the last two columns are abbreviated as follows:

O/O = Owner/Operator (can be either a private or a public entity)

G = National government

NGO = Non-governmental organisation(s)

Table 4, dealing with thwarting cyber-attacks, suggests that responsibility rests almost entirely with the owner. Only the owner can effectively control what kind of locks are on the doors, who has the keys and whether the doors remain locked.

Governments have a role in, for example, mandating levels of protection for regulated systems, including their own. They may conduct pioneering R&D and encourage the transfer of results to users everywhere; they may lend their expertise in areas such as encryption technology and penetration testing; or they may use their central position to collect, analyse and distribute information on attacks and attackers. Non-governmental organisations can also do some of these things.

The owner's responsibility is greater still in the defence of systems against insiders. As their employer, the owner has substantial control over these insiders. Governments can assist in the vetting of employees for sensitive positions by making criminal records available. These are most accessible when the system is government-owned, or when classified information or critical government-owned systems are at stake.

When the strategic objective is cooperative terminal defence, public roles are more important, although the premise here is that the participants act voluntarily. Nevertheless, governments can mediate private relationships when the public interest is at stake. Thus, civil and criminal liability must be addressed and agreements that restrict markets, reduce the safety of public systems and products or impinge on personal privacy or civil rights require some degree of monitoring. Public access and disclosure works in many cases, but a point is eventually reached where public access reduces the effectiveness of the protection the parties seek.

The choice of building intrusion-tolerant systems is entirely the owner's. Systems that incorporate enhanced safety may cost more to build, cost more to operate and be less able to benefit from technical innovation. Building it 'right' is the goal of every system designer, but success is not assured.

Table 5 addresses the capabilities needed to limit damage sustained during an attack. These requirements are highly complex, from both technical and policy viewpoints. Managing a cyber-attack in real-time is difficult. The required sensor systems, situation-assessment processes, system linkages and decision-making mechanisms

Table 5 Limiting Damage from Cyber-Attacks: Capabilities and Roles

Strategic Option	Tactical Objective	Required Capabilities	Primary Role	Secondary Role
Audit system operation	Mount adaptive defence	Battle management capability consisting of sensors embedded in information systems capable of detecting and characterising system operation	O/O	
		Templates to provide low-level assessment of system anomalies and comparison with attack signatures	O/O	G and NGO
		Communication links to higher-level analysis centres	G and NGO	
		Higher-level analytical capabilities to provide situation awareness and attack assessment	G and NGO	
		Pre-established response options	O/O	
		Assessments of thrust and goals of attacker	G and NGO	
		Ability to raise defensive capabilities in response to attack assessment (e.g., user re-authentication, quarantine new transaction requests, scanning e-mail and enclosures, backup system files, etc.)	O/O	

(Continued on next page)

Strategic Option	Tactical Objective	Required Capabilities	Primary Role	Secondary Role
	Undertake active defence	Provide near real-time warning to likely targets	O/O	G and NGO
		Enhanced collection of forensic evidence	O/O	G
		Institute packet, message, and session traces to identify attack source in near-real time	O/O	G and NGO
		Block traffic from attacker locations	O/O	
		Counterattack by blocking traffic to attacker site or account	G and NGO	
		Institute actions to seize attacking computers	G	
Pre-planned redundancy	Re-allocate system load dynamically	Maintain redundant subsystems and backup facilities	O/O	
		Reroute transactions to surviving capability	O/O	
		Simulation capability to support dynamic reconfiguration of system	O/O	

do not exist for large-scale systems.[1]

The capabilities for mounting an adaptive defence can be found in both the private and the public sector. Globally, sensors and low-level assessment are at the system-owner level, but higher-level assessment is a national function. Decision-making would be widely shared and the execution of defence decisions broadly distributed. The collection of forensic information would also be distributed, but under processes specified nationally.

Difficulties notwithstanding, local concepts of adaptive defence are possible where a number of system owners collaborate to share information on a near real-time basis. In this case, locally adaptive defence may be technically feasible, although such non-state actions are subject to the constraints imposed by the legal jurisdictions in which they might occur.

Active defence shifts more of the burden on to national government. It requires the exercise of sovereign power, and the implications of active measures will be national in their impact.

Limiting damage can also employ the dynamic re-allocation of system load, minimising the total impact of an attack by protecting priority functions and locations at the expense of others. To the extent that the design and operation of the system under attack has provided for redundant capacity, load prioritisation and capabilities to shift load in response to system stress, such approaches offer some hope. In a sense, these are an integral part of good system design, and may normally be expected from the engineering profession. The exigencies they anticipate can arise from a number of circumstances of both natural and accidental origin. They do, however, have associated costs, in terms of initial capitalisation, higher operating costs and lower system utilisation. The engineering profession is divided on the subject; some insist on 'five nines' (99.999%) reliability, while others pursue advanced technology of unproven reliability. Government regulation can also play a role, such as in requiring a minimum quality of service of regulated utilities.

The new feature that cyber-attacks introduce into the system-design process is their potentially enormous disruption. Natural events are usually limited in space and are infrequent, and accidents are usually even more local, although air transport systems and nuclear power plants can display failures of impressive proportions.

Table 6 relates to the post-attack reconstitution of a system.

Table 6 Reconstituting Systems Following Cyber-Attacks: Capabilities and Roles

Strategic Option	Tactical Objective	Required Capabilities	Primary Role	Secondary Role
Short-term reconstitution (moderate attacks)	Assess damage and implement recovery plan	Online state-of-health monitoring	O/O	
		Operational centre for recovery operations	O/O	G and NGO
		Online and up-to-date recovery plan	O/O	
	Restore system state from back-up records	Frequent back-up procedures	O/O	
		Online download from recovery centres	O/O	
		Notification of irretrievable transactions		
		Black start procedures to bring system online	O/O	
	Ration residual resources and capacity	Priority system among users	O/O	G and NGO
		Two-way communication with users	O/O	
		Ability to re-plan priorities in the light of circumstances	O/O	G and NGO

Strategic Option	Tactical Objective	Required Capabilities	Primary Role	Secondary Role
	Generate additional capacity	Collect information on off-line capacity (e.g., in maintenance, moth-balled, standby)	O/O	G and NGO
		Plan actions to activate generated capacity	O/O	G and NGO
Long-term reconstitution (severe attacks)	Stockpile long-lead items in the event of physical damage	Undertake worst-case scenario development	O/O	G and NGO
		Identify critical facilities subject to physical damage	O/O	
		Identify location of equipment and capabilities critical for repair or reconstitution	O/O	G and NGO
	Manage risk	Combine self-insurance, commercial insurance, carrier reinsurance, and federal government underwriting	O/O	G
		Record information pre- and post-attack to support claims	O/O	

This is an area where the system owner has the central role, for only the owner can establish what is operating and what is not, what reconstitution alternatives exist and how remedial measures can be effected operationally. Governments can be important in, for instance, providing back-up personnel and facilities when private resources are unavailable; assisting in the coordination of emergency responses; or providing leadership in drawing up pre-attack planning for disaster recovery. The continuity of business operation and the performance of mission-critical functions will be essential. Insurers will demand prudence, as will shareholders and the providers of financial resources.

Again, the central feature of cyber-attacks is not that they introduce a new concept of system failure and recovery, but that the scale of the problem may exceed the imagination and planning horizons of both providers and users of infrastructure services. Therefore, it is in this area that governments will be critical.

Table 7 examines the capabilities required for improving defensive performance through the lessons learnt and the design of future system enhancements. Exploitable flaws in systems need to be identified so that they can be minimised. Since owners have only a limited knowledge of their systems and their vulnerabilities, third-party assistance, such as an industry group or security organisation with experience of a wide range of systems, may be more effective. For the same reason, such third-party mechanisms will be better able to establish models of attacks and attackers, and will have a greater incentive to share lessons learnt. It is the responsibility of the owner/operator to employ independent attack teams in design reviews and system-penetration testing.

Most commercial information systems are designed to meet the owners' functional requirements, which usually involves only a minimal amount of defensive thinking. The design of weapon systems, where resistance to attack is an explicit criterion, is a better model. Yet however carefully commercial designers approach the problem, they are rarely able to match the viciousness of a dedicated attacker. The equivalent of damage control in combat systems is provided by the design of forensic data collection subsystems, which are in turn fully protected against compromise. Where the owner/operator has primary responsibility, third-party assistance is likely to be necessary.

Table 7 Improving Defensive Performance Following Cyber-Attacks: Capabilities and Roles

Strategic Option	Tactical Objective	Required Capabilities	Primary Role	Secondary Role
Pre-attack preparation	Identify exploitable flaws	Compile record of attacks on similar systems to identify known vulnerabilities	NGO	O/O
		Create models of attacks and attackers	G and NGO	O/O
		Establish independent attack teams to participate in system design reviews and to undertake penetration testing	O/O	NGO and G
		Provide a mechanism for distributing lessons learnt through the system specification process, design reviews and penetration testing to organisations facing comparable threats	NGO	O/O
	Design systems defensively	Include a defensive element in system design reviews	O/O	NGO
		Include design of forensic data collection tools and procedures in system specifications	O/O	NGO
		Include in system specifications the ability to enhance forensic data collection capabilities	O/O	NGO

(Continued on next page)

Strategic Option	Tactical Objective	Required Capabilities	Primary Role	Secondary Role
	Protect system defensive capabilities	Include in system specification the requirement that defensive capabilities be protected and that systems be hardened against the compromise of defensive capabilities by attack probes	O/O	NGO
Post-attack learning	Analyse attack forensic data	Identify critical gaps in design, testing and operation of the penetrated system	O/O	NGO
		Assess adequacy of forensic data collection tools	O/O	NGO
		Assess the trade-off between immediate solutions and more fundamental architectural changes to enhance system robustness	O/O	NGO
	Distribute results of post-attack analyses	Distribute lessons learned so that others can incorporate them into their pre-attack planning	O/O	NGO
		Use data from attacks to project the direction and speed of attack technology	NGO	O/O

A similar defensive orientation is needed to protect critical elements of a system's defensive characteristics. For example, strict need-to-know compartmentalisation principles, as practised in government security organisations, need to be applied.

After an attack, the practice should be to discover the causes for the defensive failure and to develop modifications to prevent any recurrence. In commercial organisations, the incentive is to restore the pre-attack state as soon as possible, and to recoup losses before making major investments in security. The fact that complex systems comprise large amounts of legacy, or dated, software, much of it poorly documented and often subject to less-than-adequate configuration management, further complicates the technical task of the defender.

In many cases, the safest move from a security standpoint would be to make significant changes in system architecture and operating procedures. But the cost both financially and in terms of business disruption frequently proves too great. An important role for third-party organisations is to evaluate the lessons of an attack with a view to projecting trends in attackers' capabilities.

In the long term, the central issue is the education of the engineers responsible for the design and operation of complex infrastructure systems. It will take time to introduce computer technology into older mechanical, electrical and hydraulic systems, and it will require new understanding of system complexity, especially in the way that information technology allows the 'chaining' of systems to produce entities of apparently unlimited extent. The situation is similar to the engineering experience of recent decades in the design of stealth aircraft, where aeronautical engineers found that system performance required as much attention to Maxwell's equations as to the Navier-Stokes equation and Newton's Laws of Motion.[2][3]

Chapter 4

Selecting a Strategy

Table 2, as expanded by Tables 3–7, presents a taxonomy of strategic objectives and the possible options for achieving them available to nations seeking to protect their information-dependent infrastructures. While this taxonomy cannot be proved complete with mathematical rigour, it is based on the interactions between attack and defence familiar to strategic military analyses. To the extent that the taxonomy is at least reasonably complete, it can be viewed as a 'space for solutions'. In arriving at a viable national strategy, a government needs a strategy for selecting one of the alternatives presented to meet its own technical, economic and social needs. The aim is a national strategy for cyber-defence.

A government must first identify which of its infrastructures require nationally organised protection. This focuses attention on the efficient application of national resources, protecting what is most critical and deferring what is less critical. This includes an examination of infrastructure interdependencies, since this is a point that can be exploited by an attacker. An attacker will seek to achieve the greatest possible effect with the least effort and risk. The most critical infrastructures may, for example, be those with the greatest number of interdependency relationships, rather than those with the greatest intrinsic value. While the focus of attention here is on cyber-attack, potential targets include not only systems supporting e-commerce, financial services and government services, but also the information-intensive command and control subsystems that manage physical systems such as transport, energy supply and distribution, water and the emergency services.

Central to selecting from the strategic objectives in Table 2 is the feasibility – political, technical and economic – of each. A government must, for example, assess its ability to prevent attacks on national infrastructure systems, as outlined in Table 3. This implies determining whether, now or in the future, the prevention of attacks is likely. This requires an appreciation of how such a strategy might be implemented, what it might cost, whether the leadership is prepared to pay that price and how effective it would be. The core question is whether a government feels that it can reliably achieve this strategic objective.

Similarly, an assessment is needed of the feasibility of thwarting attacks on those critical national infrastructure systems, as outlined in Table 4. That is, does the national leadership believe that, through a combination of individual and cooperative terminal defence by owners and operators, damage can be reduced to a tolerable level.

Finally, a government must assess the ability to limit damage to national infrastructure systems from those attacks that are at least partially successful, as outlined in Table 5. The government must understand how damage limitation would be accomplished; how long it might take to implement it; how much this might cost; and whether the leadership is prepared to provide adequate resources for its development and operation. What is required is cyber battle management, the ability to detect and assess the goals of an attack and to decide in near real-time which protective countermeasures to take.

Based on these assessments, the logical possibilities suggested by Figure 3 are reduced to four cases:

Case I – Defence Confident: confident of either preventing or thwarting an attack and limiting damage
In this case, the strategy should focus on preventing or thwarting an attack, with some investment in damage-limitation capability for instances where an attack cannot be avoided, the defence is not perfect and damage cannot be avoided entirely.

Case II – Light Reconstitution: confident of preventing or thwarting an attack, but not confident of damage limitation
Here, the focus is on preventing or thwarting an attack, dividing remaining resources between the short- and long-term reconstitution options.

Case III – Battle Management: not confident of preventing or thwarting an attack, but confident of limiting damage

The bulk of national investment should be directed to damage limitation. Only the easiest preventative measures need be considered. Recognising that such a course limits but does not entirely eliminate damage, some resources must also be allocated to reconstitution. The balance between damage limitation and reconstitution will depend on the degree of confidence in damage limitation. The lower that confidence, the more resources should be put into preparing for reconstitution.

Case IV – Heavy Reconstitution: lack of confidence in preventing or thwarting attack and limiting damage from an attack
This assessment requires the most drastic and far-reaching set of national actions. The strategy would suggest encouraging long-term changes in infrastructure architecture in the direction of greater local self-sufficiency, moving away from the heavy integration of infrastructures and seeking to minimise interdependencies. To the extent that a country sees itself as powerless to prevent or thwart an attack or to limit damage, planning and policies should be directed to facilitating rapid reconstitution.

However optimistic a nation is about preventing or thwarting an attack and limiting damage in Cases I and III, it would seem prudent to put at least some resources into reconstitution. Case I might be presumed to require less attention to reconstitution, since basic prevention is believed to be effective and damage limitation is expected to contain those attacks that are successful. In Cases II and III, where either prevention or damage limitation is in serious doubt, there is a greater need to prepare for reconstitution. In Case IV, a design requirement for any infrastructure is that it be easy to reconstitute rapidly.

The identification of strategic objectives is accompanied by an assessment of how quickly a government wants to be able to deal with a severe blow to its economy or security from a cyber-attack on its national infrastructure.

For convenience, the future will be considered in 5–10-year periods. One might formalise this into three situations:

Situation A – the government wishes to be prepared to deal with an infrastructure attack within the next five years
The strategy should be based on initiating defensive responses and laying the groundwork for longer-term actions. This implies a strategy that can be formulated rapidly, and focuses on actions which are

feasible to implement, and can be effective within a five-year period.

Situation B – the government sees the need to deal with infrastructure attacks, but no sooner than in 5–15 years

The strategy should focus on preparing future defensive responses. It can be more flexible, and programmes for its implementation need not be initiated immediately. The strategy can, for example, focus on longer-term actions such as security R&D, the training of security professionals and gaining a better understanding of threats and vulnerabilities.

Situation C – the government does not expect to have to face the problem of cyber-attack on its infrastructures within the foreseeable future

The strategy should be monitoring developments in defence capabilities and in threat and vulnerability assessments. An effort should be made to put the issues on the agenda of public and private decision-makers, especially for guiding the evolution of national investments in infrastructure systems to enhance their reliability and robustness under stress.

If a government decides to prepare an attack within the next five years, this does not render long-term measures inappropriate. These less urgent measures can often be cheaper in the near term since their cost can be spread over a longer period; if there is no immediate attack, longer-term measures that are slower to mature can still be effective; and even in the case of a perceived near-term threat, the technology of attack and defence will continue to develop, as will the attractiveness of the target that a nation presents to an attacker.

Having established where a country falls with respect to these four cases, as well as its time-frame for readiness, the next step is to create a national plan to implement the strategy. The details of this will depend upon three factors: the degree of public ownership of critical infrastructures; the acceptability of regulation for the infrastructures' owners and operators; and the complexity of the market structure for the provision of each critical infrastructure service.

Where there is substantial public ownership of essential national services, the strategy for their protection is an administrative function of government. The concerns of private owners will not have to be considered, but attention must be paid to the needs of the governed and to economic realities.

Where critical infrastructure is mainly in private hands but there is an acceptance of government direction, implementation of a plan of protection can be through regulation. The complexity of the market for each infrastructure service will be crucial. As complexity increases, government policy will be carried out through market forces rather than by direct technical, rate or performance regulation. When critical infrastructure is heavily in private hands and there is little tradition of government regulation, the only recourse is to depend on market forces and government persuasion to create reliable infrastructures. The governmental role will be reduced to funding research and feasibility demonstrations, and providing facilities for the collection and sharing of information on threats and vulnerabilities.

One response to the policy issues surrounding the national defence of infrastructures is that the matter should be set aside pending definitive threat assessments. Raising the issue as one of attack rather than defence enables the potential for cyber-weapons to be viewed in terms of benefits received rather than of costs imposed. The skills needed to mount a cyber-attack, the degree and type of target planning required, the relationship between cyber-weapons and conventional military capabilities and the scenarios under which such attacks might be initiated can be examined from a different perspective.

Different public policy models can be adopted in structuring a response to threats to infrastructure according to national goals and priorities. Emphasising the need to deal with life-threatening events suggests focusing on early detection and the isolation of attacks. Where maintaining access to shared resources is central, fairness and quality of service are paramount. The protection of property rights and the maintenance of public order suggest directing attention to legal models dealing with civil and criminal justice. Which of these is most effective will vary according to the particular infrastructure being protected.[1]

Chapter 5

Strategic Options

In this chapter, the strategic framework in Chapter 4 is applied to the US and the UK to examine its utility. The aim is to see how the conceptual structure can be used in specific circumstances, as well as to examine the response of two major nations, both highly dependent on their automated and interconnected national infrastructures, to concerns over cyber-attack.

The United States
Strategy
In the US, official recognition of the threat was marked by a Presidential Executive Order issued in mid-1996.[1] The US administration has identified eight critical infrastructures: transport, oil and gas production and storage, water supply, emergency services, government services, banking and finance, electrical power, and information and communication. There are, of course, other important infrastructures that build on these, for example health care, food supply and waste disposal. Identifying critical infrastructures requires establishing what failures have the greatest impact in the shortest time. Analyses of accidents, natural disasters, strikes and civil disturbances can be helpful, although such 'natural experiments' lack some of the purposely exploited correlation effects of well-planned malevolence. Such events do, however, shed light on infrastructure interdependencies.[2]

It does not appear likely that preventing an attack will be feasible in the near term. Identifying an attacker is a difficult and labour-intensive process, so the threat of punishment is unlikely yet to act as a deterrent.[3] Nor is there, in view of the rapidly changing nature of attack technology, adequate understanding of warning indicators of an information attack on which a pre-emption strategy could be based. Establishing standards for behaviour in cyberspace is also not a near-term prospect. Hacking and virus writing are popular activities, and cyber-crime is increasing.

Thwarting attacks to prevent damage is seen as technically feasible and is the focus of active R&D; a large number of commercial products are available in computer and network security.[4] The need for this has been stimulated by growing concerns over privacy and the security of electronic commerce, especially in view of cases where substantial financial losses have occurred.[5]

With respect to the possible imminence of a cyber-attack, it was the judgement of the President's Commission on Critical Infrastructure Protection (PCCIP), validated by Presidential Decision Directive 63 (PDD-63), that it would be prudent for the US to be prepared to deal with such an attack.[6] The PCCIP report and PDD-63 call for a Full Operational Capability (FOC) for the cyber-defence of critical infrastructures within five years. The official target date is December 2003.[7]

Battle management in cyberspace is far from a reality. We do not understand the basic feasibility issues. The gigabyte network research community is working to understand the features of large-scale network traffic.[8] However, virus detection is making good progress.[9] Cyberspace surveillance and linking network intrusion-detection systems is politically and legally complex. At present, both personal and business privacy groups see such surveillance as part of the problem, not part of the solution. Given the US government's target date, damage limitation cannot be a basis for a national strategy in the near term.[10] From this, and as defined in Chapter 4, the US is a Case II nation.

A strategy for the US should be to focus the bulk of its efforts on thwarting attacks to prevent damage through public and private initiatives. Remaining national resources should be used for emergency management and providing assistance in short-term reconstitution efforts.

The official position of the US – that it should be prepared for a serious attack in the near term – suggests that work should start on the eight infrastructures identified in PDD-63 immediately if the US is to meet its target. As previously noted, this short-term aim should not exclude actions that can only be effective in the longer term. But the framework underlines the issue of urgency and its consequent impact on resource-allocation priorities.

Table 4 shows the three strategic options available for thwarting cyber-attacks: individual terminal defence, cooperative terminal defence and intrusion-tolerant systems. Those selected must be able to meet the requirement of full operational capability within five years. This rules out relying on intrusion-tolerant systems, since they are not currently available and it would be a risk to count on their development and commercial deployment in the limited time available. The same argument applies to cooperative measures because so many organisations must be linked in to effective working groups. In the short term, of course, it is possible to pool information and penetration-test capabilities and establish consumer cooperatives. However, government concerns over anti-competitive practices and individual organisations' sensitivity to the protection of intellectual property and their market position will slow the near-term application of this strategic option. This leaves individual terminal defence as the only clear and immediate route.

Table 4 further indicates that the primary role in implementing this strategy is played by the owner-operator. Outside organisations can audit incoming traffic for suspicious activity, carry out penetration testing and audit the effectiveness of corrective measures. To defend against insiders, there is a possible role for government in vetting employees, since governments may have information of potential importance. And governments are typically the only entities able to document and control system interdependencies.

Since terminal defence cannot be assured in all cases, the strategy for a Case II country should include assisting reconstitution. The less effective the terminal defence, the more prudent it is to invest in reconstitution. Table 6 shows what options are available. Given the essentially private nature of most infrastructure in the US, reconstitution is, like defence, primarily an owner's responsibility. But a number of government and non-governmental organisations can assist. Short-term actions include a 'clearing house' role in assessing damage, establishing priorities to restore service in the most effective way possible and relaxing regulations to allow additional capacity to be brought online temporarily.

These short-term reconstitution actions are where outside

intervention is most welcome by private entities. But for longer-term intervention the responsibility should rest heavily with the private owners. They are responsible for investing in the maintenance and expansion of their systems, and hence are in the best position to factor losses from attacks into capital investment plans.

Implementation

The starting point for implementation is to recognise that infrastructures in the US are generally privately owned, although there is substantial government involvement in areas such as air and marine navigation, air-traffic control, hydroelectric power and regional water management. Thus, while the majority of infrastructure assets are in private hands, the government can display its commitment to infrastructure protection through its management of those systems under its direct control. Government also has an opportunity to influence infrastructure operations through its procurements in locations where it is a major customer. Especially heavy concentrations of federal influence are found, for example, in areas of major military importance, such as bases and ports.

Regulation to protect the public interest has a long history in the US, particularly to reduce monopoly power in the late nineteenth and early twentieth centuries. More recently, however, the regulation of markets and the imposition of technical standards has come to be seen as economically inefficient and as inhibiting technical and business innovation. This view notwithstanding, there is still significant regulation over public safety in transport and food and drugs, in assuring equitable access to telecommunications services, in the protection of financial markets against fraud and in the protection of the environment. Monopolies exist in local markets, such as in cable TV distribution systems, telephone services and electrical power transmission and distribution.

Therefore, the pattern of regulation in the US is mixed. But when disasters occur the public reaction is usually to ask why their government did not act sooner and more vigorously.

Placing primary responsibility on owners has the advantage of greater efficiency and less regulatory intervention in competitive markets. On the other hand, placing the responsibility for protection on actors in highly competitive markets carries the risk that concerns beyond 'normal business losses' will be ignored. The question is then how to cause private entities to act in the public interest when the threat of cyber-attack is poorly defined. There are several approaches that can encourage voluntary action. First, as more cyber-attacks and cyber-accidents occur, as well as system-wide failures due to natural events, the potential for major impacts becomes better defined. Executive branch rhetoric plays an important role, as does its commitment of resources, for example to computer and network security R&D. Government hearings related to proposed legislation, workshops involving regulated industries or government contractors and contractual awards with their accompanying news releases can all serve to keep the issue in the public eye. Tax policies directed to areas of assessed need can be used. Infrastructure failures, such as those mentioned earlier, help in a perverse way. A current rallying cry in the US is 'Avoid an Electronic Pearl Harbor'.

Infrastructures that are direct public responsibilities include defence and intelligence infrastructures and those for government services such as the Social Security Administration, health-care insurance and the law-enforcement and criminal-justice systems. There are also varying degrees of public participation in particular industries, for example hydroelectric power and regional water distribution.

Regulators are concerned with assuring the stability and fairness of financial markets, equitable access to telecommunications services and reliable, affordable electric power. Regardless of the popular rhetoric against regulation and for the free market, there is still a regulatory component of public policy based on the public's demand for safety, fairness and accountability. These may not be the preferred regulatory tools of policymakers, but they are available should private efforts in providing essential protection to the public be judged lacking. Regulation and legislation can have a deterrent effect, causing industries to modify their behaviour to prevent stronger government intervention.

A more powerful case for regulation derives from the possible need for private defensive actions that go beyond the dictates of good business practice. Making such measures universally applicable will level the domestic playing-field, but may not help US competitiveness globally, at least until there is global acceptance of the need for such protection. Another possible regulatory role would be to require independent testing or certification of private terminal defence and reconstitution efforts. An analogy is the mandated posting of privacy policies governing the use of personal information by private organisations.[11]

The US supports cooperation among private entities, but typically requires that protection of the public against monopoly power be maintained. Thus, the activities of, for example, the Internet Engineering Task Force (IETF), the Internet Corporation for Assigned Names and Numbers (ICANN) and open industry groups that do not act in restraint of trade are encouraged. The government frequently assists in the formation of such groups, as it did to enhance network security through the Computer Emergency Response Team Coordination Center at Carnegie Mellon University. Various government agencies also support pre-competitive R&D in system security and the establishment of technical standards.

The defence of information systems and the understanding of offensive capabilities interact, as there is only a short distance between the two. The US, by virtue of its advanced state of commercial and military development of information technology, has de facto capabilities in offensive information warfare.[12] Reports of as many as 30 nations establishing information-warfare activities suggest that few are ready to abjure information weapons without a better understanding of their potential.[13] Reports of activities directed against Serbia during the NATO intervention in Kosovo in 1999 support the view that defence establishments are exploring the potential of information operations.[14] While an information-warfare 'arms race' is undesirable, offence–defence balances will emerge as factors in assessing national strategic postures, to the extent that offensive cyber-attack potentials are recognised.

The United Kingdom
Strategy
The UK's level of technological development is roughly comparable to that of the US, and hence the targets it offers attackers are equally attractive. They may, in fact, be more attractive since the compact nature of the UK can make the impact of a successful attack more significant.[15]

The Home Office identifies telecommunications, energy, financial services, transport, central government, water and sewerage, health services and emergency services as vital sectors.[16] A more detailed list is provided as part of the government's specification of industries and services eligible for priority access to fuel during the September 2000 petrol-delivery crisis. These are: the emergency services, the armed forces, health and social workers, the food industry, agriculture, veterinary and animal welfare, essential workers at nuclear sites, water, sewerage and drainage, fuel and energy suppliers, public transport, licensed taxis, coast guards and lifeboat crews, airport and airline workers, post, media and telecommunications workers, central and local-government workers, essential financial-services staff, including those involved in the delivery of cash and bank drafts, prison staff, refuse collection and industrial waste, funeral services, special schools and colleges for the disabled and essential foreign diplomatic workers.[17]

In the near term, preventing an attack is no more likely to be feasible in the UK than in the US. The same labour-intensive process of being able to identify an attacker in order to deter one must be employed. Indications and warnings of a reliable pre-emptive response are as difficult in terms of both data collection and analysis for the UK as for the US. And both nations suffer under the current state of worldwide cyber-ethics. But in the longer term, it is not unreasonable to believe that normative behaviour in cyberspace can change should the current state of disorder become unacceptable to enough users.

Thwarting attacks is seen as technically feasible. It is the goal of the government to defend the critical national infrastructure against electronic attack.[18] The same commercial computer and network security products are available as in the US.[19]

The UK's assessment is that, while it does not see the need to be prepared for an electronic attack on its national infrastructure within the next five years, it does not assess the need to be so remote as to make government attention unnecessary.[20] This would seem to put the matter into the 5–15-year category.

For the same reason as in the US, battle management in cyberspace is far from a reality. Network security tools that allow the recording of input packet traffic[21] for off-line analysis to detect attack signatures are commercially available, but they are computationally intensive, and the fact that this is done off-line does not allow the short response time that would presumably be required for real-time damage limitation. This is a fundamental problem for all damage-limitation strategies, although continuing R&D progress can be expected to reduce the response time. Virus detection is a significant part of the commercial security market, and R&D on the automatic detection of new viruses and semi-automated responses is an important focus. For these reasons, damage limitation is not under consideration, although it is an active R&D area and has been successful in reducing telephone fraud. The then home secretary Jack Straw stated in parliament that the government 'is enhancing warning and incident response arrangements. For these reasons the National Infrastructure Security Co-ordination Centre (NISCC) has been established as a single point of contact on electronic attack issues for those in the national infrastructure and to enhance co-ordination of the relevant departments and agencies working in this area'.[22] However, the NISCC is not, by its nature, able to provide real-time response, and to date its warnings, such as for the e-mailed Love Bug virus during 2000, were issued after most had experienced the attack first-hand.

Thus the UK, like the US, is a 'Case II' country: The UK should focus the bulk of its efforts on thwarting attacks to prevent damage through public and private initiatives. Remaining national resources should be used for emergency management and providing assistance in short-term reconstitution efforts.

But unlike the US with its five-year target, the UK view is that a serious cyber-attack on its national infrastructure is further off. Hence its strategic response can be rather different. While the UK's long-term objectives, primarily to prevent an attack or limit damage from an attack, but with some attention to reconstitution, are the same as in the US, the time to achieve these objectives is significantly greater for the UK. This opens up a wider set of strategic options.

If a severe attack was considered imminent, the UK would face the same options as the US: to encourage individual terminal defence and short-term reconstitution. Since these are largely responsibilities of infrastructure owners, market forces will drive the degree to which they might be implemented, which is clearly the policy preference of the UK. There are, nevertheless, secondary roles for government, as suggested in Table 4. Making these actions a high priority would provide a hedging component to an overall UK strategy. There is some evidence that the UK is moving in this direction.[23]

Of the five remaining strategic options, cooperative terminal defence in Table 4 offers the lowest political and technical risk. This contributes directly to the UK's goal of protection. It requires no new technical discoveries, and its effectiveness will increase as the number of organisations and nations participating in cooperative defence increases.

As with individual terminal defence and short-term reconstitution, the primary responsibility for cooperative terminal defence rests with infrastructure owners. Therefore, it will be implemented through the voluntary actions of service providers in direct proportion to its value in supporting business objectives. There are important, albeit secondary, roles for government. These include assisting the collecting and sharing of attack-related information and the investigation of infrastructure failures to prevent their recurrence, and participating in the development of industry best practices and standards for system security. As an alliance-builder against common adversaries, cooperative terminal defence will be a familiar role for government. Success in mobilising collective action against violators of order in cyberspace might in the longer term improve the global capability to deter such violations and improve the behaviour of nations and their citizens in the global information realm.

The two final strategic options are technical in nature and are likely to require the longest time for research, development, testing and deployment. These are intrusion-tolerant systems and near real-time systems for attack warning and attack assessment. If these are at all feasible, they are unlikely to play a role in the defence of systems until some time in the future. Thus they represent areas to monitor but not to rely on for the protection of essential services.[24]

Implementation

British governments have recently placed great emphasis on privatising national infrastructures. The outsourcing of support functions by UK government departments and their dependence on commercial software is also probably more extensive than in the US. So long as it remains government policy to leave the bulk of the UK's national infrastructure in private hands, improving its protection will be a matter for contract negotiation rather than direct government decision.[25]

Infrastructure regulation in the UK operates on two levels. One derives from membership in the European Union, and the other is at the domestic level to protect taxpayers and markets from abuses. While both have the public good as their goal, the inevitable delay in developing European legislation affects the degree to which the UK can develop and enact underpinning legislation of its own.[26]

UK national infrastructures typically involve fewer companies in each sub-market than in the US, due partly to the size difference between the two countries, and partly to the UK's privatisation of a few large government entities. For example, British Telecom-munications plc still has 70% of the long-distance market and there is a single supplier, the National Grid Corporation, for electric power transmission in England and Wales, and one, Scottish Electric, for Scotland. There are 14 regional distribution companies for electric power and roughly 200 licensed telephone companies.[27]

The security impact of the number of independent companies that together make up an infrastructure system cuts both ways. With fewer companies there are fewer points of management control over the parts of the infrastructure and hence fewer points of contact for organisations intent on promulgating security enhancements. Also since each independent company has interfaces with its neighbours, there are fewer technical and management interfaces where things can go wrong or communications misunderstood. On the other hand, with fewer decision makers, their decisions impact a larger fraction of the total infrastructure and when their decisions are faulty, or their management practices ineffective, the larger is the fraction of the infrastructure that is affected. Thus, the issue of relative numbers of independent companies is not to suggest that one way of organising an infrastructure is superior to the other. Instead it is to suggest that from a security perspective, the types of technical and management problems will be different.

Like the US, the UK has de facto capabilities in offensive information warfare. And like the US, it is presumably unlikely to forgo its options with respect to information warfare and information weapons pending a clearer understanding of their capabilities and limitations.

Chapter 6

Protecting Infrastructures in the US and the UK

The United States

In the US, infrastructure protection is seen as one of several national security concerns addressed under the rubric of 'homeland defence', a category that includes national missile defence, the countering of foreign intelligence collection, domestic preparedness against weapons of mass destruction and national security emergency preparedness. National policy for infrastructure protection was first established by PDD-63. This directive called for the creation of a National Plan for Information Systems Protection.[1] The focus of the plan was a management structure through which the US government could address the problem via actions that it could take directly and initiatives undertaken jointly with the private sector.

Some of the measures initiated by the Clinton administration have continued under the Bush administration, although under different management and supervision arrangements. A comprehensive report is available on the status of federal critical infrastructure protection activities as of January 2001.[2] The Bush administration's National Security Presidential Directive–1 reaffirmed the importance of the issue and continued to link the supervision of infrastructure protection efforts with those for counter-terrorism. The president's National Security Advisor, Condoleezza Rice, noted on 23 March 2001: 'Corrupt those [IT] networks and you disrupt this nation. We can't afford to take [IT] for granted. Today the cybereconomy is the economy.'[3]

Following the terrorist attacks of 11 September 2001, the Bush administration formally established an Office of Homeland Security in the executive office of the president. It further defined its approach to critical infrastructure protection in Executive Order 13231.[4] The executive order establishes the policy of the US to protect information systems for critical infrastructure, and thereby help protect the people, the economy, essential human and government services and national security. It seeks to ensure that any disruption is infrequent, of minimal duration and causes the least damage possible.

The President's Critical Infrastructure Protection Board has been established to coordinate government actions taken by executive branch departments and agencies, and to continue the supervisory role for specific critical infrastructures previously assigned to various departments and agencies. The board consists of 25 members representing executive branch departments and agencies. The board functions through ten standing committees responsible for: private sector and state and local government outreach; the security of executive branch information systems; national security systems; incident response coordination; research and development; national security and emergency preparedness communications; physical security; infrastructure interdependencies; international affairs; and the financial and banking information infrastructure. The board is responsible for proposing a National Plan or plans for critical infrastructure protection. In coordination with the Office of Homeland Security, the board is instructed to make recommendations to the Office of Management and Budget (OMB) on those parts of executive branch department and agency budgets that are relevant to critical infrastructure protection. The board is also assigned authority to ask various federal departments and agencies to include in their budget requests to the OMB funding for research and demonstration projects related to critical infrastructure protection. The chair of the board reports to three individuals: the assistant to the president for national security affairs on national security-related issues; the director of the Office of Homeland Security on issues related to homeland security; and the official responsible for combating terrorism.

On 14 February, 2003 the President released a new strategic plan that reflected both progress on the problem to date and the priorities as seen by the new administration.[5] The plan lays out five priorities, each with a number of major initiatives and actions identified. These five priorities are: a national cyberspace security response system; a national cyberspace security threat and vulnerability reduction programme; a national cyberspace security awareness and training programme; securing government cyberspace; and national security and international cyberspace security cooperation. The major change between this and the earlier plan is that the new Department of Homeland Security has the responsibility for overseeing its implementation instead of the widely distributed responsibilities of a number of executive branch departments coordinated by the Executive Office of the President. The preparation of this strategic plan was aided by contributions from the owners and operators of the nation's various critical infrastructure sectors. These sector inputs were provided through the auspices of the Partnership for Critical Infrastructure Security, a group established to coordinate cross-sector initiatives and to complement public-private efforts.[6]

The federal government is assisted by two advisory groups. One, the president's National Security Telecommunications Advisory Panel (NSTAC), is concerned with the security and continuity of systems essential for national security and emergency preparedness.[7] The National Infrastructure Advisory Council (NIAC) is concerned with the security of information systems of critical infrastructures supporting the economy: banking and finance, energy, transport, manufacturing and emergency government services. Its members are drawn from the private sector, academia and state and local government.

Beyond boards and committees, the organisation in the federal government that has critical infrastructure protection as its full-time responsibility is the Critical Infrastructure Assurance Office (CIAO).[8] The CIAO coordinates national policy planning and outreach initiatives with private industry and assists federal agencies in analysing their critical infrastructure dependencies and interdependencies. It works to raise national awareness across industry sectors; to influence corporate information assurance policy; to promote market solutions for more robust cyber-security; to identify and address statutory and regulatory issues that potentially discourage or undermine business initiatives; and to assist voluntary efforts at enhancing critical infrastructure assurance.

The National Infrastructure Protection Center (NIPC) serves as a focus for critical infrastructure threat assessment, warning, vulnerability and law-enforcement investigation and response.[9] Its mission is

Table 8 Information Sharing and Analysis Centres for Enhancing Infrastructure Protection

Infrastructure	Lead agency	Sector ISAC	Purpose
Banking and finance	Department of the Treasury	Financial Services ISAC	Provide early warning of cyber-attack
Electric power	Department of Energy	North American Electric Reliability Council	Train employees to recognise and report acts of physical and electronic sabotage
Emergency services			
Fire and rescue	Federal Emergency Management Agency	National Fire Academy	Research fire-related threats; collect and publish data from local fire departments
Law enforcement	Federal Bureau of Investigation	National Communications System	Provide access to time-sensitive attack warning on computing and communications infrastructure
Public health	Department of Health and Human Resources	To be determined	To be determined
Information	Department of Commerce	Information Technology Association of America	Build network for exchanging information about electronic threats and countermeasures
Telecommunications	Department of Commerce	National Coordinating Center for Telecommunications	Create and share information about vulnerabilities, threats and outages
Oil and gas	Department of Energy	National Petroleum Council	Create an ISAC

Infrastructure	Lead agency	Sector ISAC	Purpose
Transportation			
Surface	Department of Transportation	Association of American Railroads	Create an ISAC
Air	Department of Transportation	To be determined	To be determined
Water	Environmental Protection Agency	Association of Metropolitan Water	Establish a network to broadcast alerts and information on vulnerabilities and crisis response

to detect, deter, assess, warn and investigate unlawful acts involving computer and information technologies and unlawful acts, both physical and cyber, that threaten or target critical infrastructures; manage computer intrusion investigations; support law enforcement, counter-terrorism and foreign counter-intelligence missions related to cyber-crimes and intrusion; support national security authorities when unlawful acts go beyond crime and are foreign-sponsored attacks on US interests; and coordinate training for cyber-investigations and infrastructure protection in government and the private sector.

To avoid imposing costs, the US policy has been to favour voluntary public–private partnerships between the federal government and the private sector over regulation. Each infrastructure sector has been encouraged to establish an Information Sharing and Analysis Center (ISAC) for critical infrastructure protection. The aim is that private-sector cooperation on assessing threats and sharing information on the reduction of vulnerabilities and on the establishment of best security practices can over the long term result in more secure systems, and provide a basis for cooperation in an emergency. On the government side, each lead agency designates a senior official to be a point of contact with a corresponding private-sector area coordinator. Table 8 shows the kind of activities that have been implemented to date.[10]

Ten programmes are defined in the current version of the National Plan:

1. Identify critical infrastructure assets and interdependencies, and address vulnerabilities
2. Detect attacks and unauthorised intrusions
3. Develop robust intelligence and law-enforcement capabilities
4. Share attack warnings and information
5. Create capabilities for response, reconstitution and recovery
6. Enhance research and development in support of programmes 1–5
7. Train and employ adequate numbers of information-security specialists
8. Outreach to make Americans aware of the need for improved cyber-security
9. Adopt legislation and appropriations in support of programmes 1–8

10. Ensure protection of civil rights, rights to privacy and protection of proprietary data

The plan specifies a series of programme milestones. Subsequent versions are expected to include reports on progress.

In comparing this set of activities with the strategy suggested in Chapter 5, one can distinguish between those things that the government does on its own behalf as an owner/operator of internal infrastructure systems, and those where it is acting more widely on behalf of the country. The first five programmes are for the most part directed to the former, while the last five are directed to the latter.

Acting on its own behalf, the plan's goals are consistent with the strategy suggested here. They focus on individual terminal defence and even attempt to go beyond that in terms of cooperation, at least among government agencies. However, when one examines the milestones in more detail, it becomes apparent that they are not consistent with the schedule mandated by PDD-63, that is, Full Operational Capability (FOC) by the end of 2003. The IOC (Initial Operational Capability) and FOC called for in PDD-63 are defined functionally: 'to protect our nation's critical infrastructures from intentional acts that would significantly diminish the abilities of the Federal Government to perform essential national security missions and to ensure the general public health and safety'. But the plan does not define IOC and FOC in terms that enable one to decide whether they have been achieved. Instead, the plan leaves this to each agency. Given the lack of uniformity of protection across infrastructures, assessing completion will be difficult.

From the standpoint of the protection of the nation as a whole, the plan is not consistent with the schedule called for in PDD-63. Programmes 6–9 call for R&D to find solutions, training that involves filling a personnel pipeline, outreach to convince the country there is a problem and enacting legislation that involves traditional processes and numerous checks and balances. These are not tasks that lead to immediate solutions.

While many of the programmes in the national plan are still in their early stages and organisational arrangements are in flux, it is possible to make some observations relating to implementation:

*   The private sector looks with scepticism on public–private partnerships, seeing them as regulation and unfunded mandates.

- The interface between law enforcement agencies as first responders and the national security establishment that must deal with state-supported attacks is complex and can impede responses in urgent situations.
- Protecting infrastructures is a mixture of incompatible objectives: on the one hand the protection of user privacy, and on the other enhanced capabilities for domestic wiretapping, the control of encryption technology and intrusive monitoring of data transmissions. The current concern about the Echelon and Carnivore systems is a case in point.[11]
- Funding for critical-infrastructure protection programmes has been slow to materialise, although the General Accounting Office is critical of the federal government's performance in computer and network security.
- Organising national programmes around 'stovepipe' definitions of infrastructures makes addressing interdependency issues difficult. Regulatory policies mandate open entry into deregulated industries, but this encourages the limitless chaining of networks into ever more complex structures and requires open access to operational details that assists the entry of attackers.
- Federal procurement policy encourages the use of commercial off-the-shelf software. Such software, with its widely-known security flaws, has provided the entry point for virtually all recent virus and distributed denial-of-service attacks on information systems.
- International initiatives are required since the problems of shared cyber-systems and their cyber-ills are not purely domestic. It is not clear if there is a single point in the US responsible for monitoring progress in enhancing the protection of its critical infrastructures. Since the US lacks measures to express the robustness of its infrastructure systems, it is difficult to know whether critical infrastructures are becoming more or less robust as a result of government and private initiatives and new technology.[12]

These are not fatal flaws. However, they do highlight problems that could slow the process of reducing the vulnerability of infrastructures.

The United Kingdom

An important factor in the UK's infrastructure protection is the Information Age Government initiative, as well as national security concerns about information-warfare attacks. The objective of the initiative is to make the British government a global exemplar in its use of information and communication technologies.[13] There are a number of elements to this:

(a)   An Office of Government Commerce;

(b)   Security for such procurement processes through the use of a public key infrastructure. The process for defence e-commerce procurements is being developed under the aegis of the Communications-Electronic Security Group.

(c)   An Electronic Communications Bill to ensure that government departments give equivalence to written and digital documents.

(d)   The transfer of experience of business-process change from the private to the public sector through the Centre for Management and Policy Studies in the Cabinet Office.

(e)   The electronic delivery of government services as outlined in the Modernising Government White Paper. The programme is managed by the Central IT Unit that reports to the Office of the e-Envoy.

(f)   Plans for access to government services through a portal site; private keys are planned for physical delivery in 'software wallets';

(g)   A White Paper on the Future Management of the Crown Copyright that has led to the establishment of an Information Assets Register providing an electronic gateway to government material.

(h)   A set of 15 'commitments' that provide further detail on implementation of the above objectives.

With such an aggressive programme to recast government processes around information technology, infrastructure protection is clearly a central concern. UK planning for infrastructure protection benefited from Y2K measures that required all users of information technology, public and private, to review the software on which their operations depended.[14] This also required system operators to uncover interdependencies, all of which constituted a valuable review of infrastructure operations nationally.

In December 1999, the NISCC was established to coordinate policy implementation and extend existing work on protecting critical national infrastructure within government departments and the private sector from electronic attack. The management board consists of representatives of the Home Office, the Cabinet Office, Ministry of Defence (MoD), the CESG (a division of the government monitoring centre GCHQ), the security services and the police. Its founding statement notes that it 'will coordinate and develop work in a number of government departments and agencies and in the private sector. This will include developing arrangements to monitor and increase awareness of the threat, to defend against it and to react to actual attacks'.[15]

The NISCC operates the Unified Incident Reporting and Alert Scheme (UNIRAS), which provides a central point for reporting any potential threat. It then distributes security alerts to information system operators, using the Government Secure Intranet to those departments connected to it or via e-mail, telephone or other means as available.[16] UNIRAS operates with support from the Central Incident Recording Reporting and Alert System (CIRRAS) of the Central Computer and Telecommunications Agency (CCTA). UNIRAS handles security incidents, including natural disasters, wilful damage, theft, misuse of resources, viruses, hacking, personnel errors, and personnel shortages. CIRRAS maintains databases of incidents, weaknesses, intelligence, alert tracking, departmental contacts, vendors, experts, IT security products and suppliers.[17] A recent report raises questions of the availability of information from UNIRAS, noting that it has not recorded a single case of successful intrusion since it was set up in 1992, compared to the hundreds of thousands of intrusions reported by the comparable US system operated by the CERT Coordination Center.[18]

The National Criminal Intelligence Service published a threat assessment of crime related to computer networks, Project Trawler, in June 1999.[19] However, problems in data collection have been noted. Police forces are not required to report or maintain records of complaints and prosecutions under the Computer Misuse Act. Even when statistics are available, some government departments have refused permission to use the information.[20]

Standards for information security management are available as BS 7799. This standard was prepared by the British Standards Institution BSI/DISC committee, whose members include a wide range of concerned organisations.[21] BS 7799 sets out a number of guiding principles, some of which are essential from a legislative viewpoint, such as data protection and privacy of personal information and safeguarding organisational information. Other controls fall under the category of best practice, such as business continuity management and information security education and training. The IT Security Evaluation and Certification (ITSEC) scheme, operational since May 1991, is managed by the Department of Trade and Industry (DTI) and CESG. It provides a way of identifying independently-tested, assured computer security products.[22] All UK government departments are required, as a minimum, to comply with BS 7799.[23]

CESG serves as a technical authority for the government: it helps define information security policy, offers consultant services to users in the public and private sector on the implementation of that policy, develops cryptographic products for government use, assists commercial organisations to develop cryptographic products suitable for government use and provides training courses and consumer goods for the government's cryptographic products and systems. CESG operates on a cost-recovery basis for customer-specific products. While its customers are mainly departments and agencies of the government and British armed forces, its range of customers has increased to include non-governmental public bodies, other public-sector bodies and police forces in the UK. It maintains contacts with UK industry and commerce. CESG is subject to the same parliamentary and governmental supervision as GCHQ.[24] In a related development, the Defence Evaluation and Research Agency (DERA) was privatised in April 2001. This allows aspects of its work, including that on information assurance, to be available to the commercial sector. DERA has undertaken contracts for industry to improve e-commerce information security.

In March 2000, the Information Assurance Advisory Council (IAAC) was launched. This private-sector organisation is intended to help bridge the gap between the public sector, represented by the NISCC, and the private sector. The IAAC is in some ways an experiment in how public- and private-sector information will be exchanged. On the public side, the issues relate to what information the government can legally provide in view of its mission responsibilities. For the private sector, the question is how far it is willing to go in sharing proprietary information and information on its vulnerabilities. The IAAC has some features in common with the US ISACs.

Part of the UK's response to the problem of protecting information systems has been to create a legal framework. There are a number of elements:

(a) The Telecommunications (Fraud) Act 1997 amended the 1984 Act to make provision for fraud in the use of the telecommunications system and to increase the penalties for fraud.[25]

(b) The Data Protection Act 1998 regulates the processing of information relating to individuals, including the obtaining, holding, use or disclosure of such information.

(c) The Electronic Communications Bill 2000 established cryptography and digital signatures as a part of the legal framework to support e-commerce. The Alliance for Electronic Business has developed a non-statutory self-regulatory proposal, known as a T-Scheme, that would operate as a not-for-profit limited company.[26]

(d) The Regulation of Investigatory Powers Bill, introduced to parliament on 9 May 2000, provides a new statutory basis for the authorisation and use by the security and intelligence agencies, law enforcement and other public authorities of covert surveillance, agents, informants, undercover officers and communications-interception techniques.[27]

(e) The Terrorism Act 2000 makes the deliberate interference in or disruption of electronic systems a criminal act.

The British government supports initiatives in existing international forums. These include G8 discussions related to criminal activities, Organisation for Economic Cooperation and Development (OECD) security standards and other international standards activities. The MoD and the security services maintain close relations with their US counterparts and other bilateral arrangements.

These efforts notwithstanding, a survey sponsored by the DTI in 2000 showed that, of the organisations responding, 60% had suffered an information-security breach in the past two years; the seriousness of unauthorised activities was assessed as between 'very' and 'extremely' serious; 86% of the organisations had no formally-defined security policy; 83% of these were not aware of BS 7799; and 41% had neither carried out a risk assessment, nor planned to do so.[28]

A national R&D agenda related to information assurance is at an early stage. Several university research centres provide skilled personnel and research results.[29] Whereas the technical community in the US feels that R&D is critical to addressing the problems of information assurance, this seems to be less so in the UK. While applied research in information assurance within the military community has been undertaken for many years, it is only recently that this has been made available to industry.[30] High-speed R&D networks serve as research testbeds and as a critical facility for training personnel in advanced networking.[31] As part of the government's Information Age Government initiative, pressure is being applied to telecommunications companies to accelerate the roll-out of high-speed networks.

Educational initiatives are also in an early stage of development. A number of government departments offer specialist training, and there are undergraduate courses in computer science. The needs of e-business are creating increased interest in graduate programmes, both in computer science and in enterprise information systems. However, fewer universities offer postgraduate education in computer security, compared with other aspects of e-business. Academic research in this topic is limited to a handful of universities, whereas most conduct research in other aspects of computer science.

Comparing the current UK critical national infrastructure activities with the suggestions presented in this paper, there are a number of points of congruence. The threat of attack is not seen as immediate, so longer-term actions, such as establishing a high-level structure for coordinating public and private-sector actions, creating the necessary authorities through legislation and writing and promulgating security standards and best practices, are appropriate.

However, activities do not appear to take advantage of the time available, whether in R&D, in assessing the need to match the long-term training of security professionals to the needs of an information-dominated society or in international initiatives. Academic R&D is particularly important because it produces the research grounding to be able to respond to increasingly powerful information attackers and expands the pool of trained personnel. International initiatives are critical to dealing with disorder in cyberspace. Experience shows that targets and attackers are often not in the same legal jurisdiction, and that worldwide cooperation is essential. Since reaching and implementing international agreements is a slow process, as is the development of an R&D and technical personnel base, the sooner a start is made, the better the use that can be made of the time available. But because policy emphasises 'making the UK the best place to do e-business', resources are directed towards promoting the e-business agenda rather than to security concerns.[32]

The UK government's policy to reorientate its operation around networked information technology is an additional consideration. Instead of increasing the robustness of its current infrastructures, it proposes to build entirely new information-based infrastructures around technology known to be untrustworthy. Furthermore, both government and the public are reluctant to adopt technologies that could lead to the introduction of a national identity card.

Chapter 7

The Broader Applicability of the Strategic Framework

This chapter applies the framework more extensively, although in much less detail, to the other countries of the world. In doing so, the aim is to describe the state of critical infrastructure-protection concerns elsewhere, and to test the applicability of the framework beyond the UK and US.

For this purpose, the world can be divided into four categories of countries and infrastructure owners and operators that have, or who may be expected to have, concerns over critical-infrastructure protection. It is important to keep in mind that, in view of the internationally networked nature of several IT-based infrastructures, problems in almost any country can also become the problems of others.

The first category covers the technically and economically advanced countries, which basically means the members of the OECD and a few other countries with economies at similar levels. There are approximately 35–40 countries in this category. Some, notably the Nordic countries, may be as dependent as the US and the UK on IT-based infrastructures. These countries (Denmark, Finland, Iceland, Norway and Sweden) form the most 'wired' region in the world on a per-capita basis. By some measures Sweden, Norway and Denmark rank first, second and third, with the US in fourth place.[1] Most others are less dependent but their dependency is increasing, and they are extensively networked with the rest of the world. These countries typically have national telephone, mobile phone and Internet penetrations of 30% or more.

The second category includes former communist and less

developed countries (LDCs), and some small, wealthy countries that cannot match either the interconnectivity or the indigenous technological strengths of the countries in the first category. Countries in the latter group acquire almost their entire IT-based infrastructure from foreign sources.[2] There may be roughly another 30–35 countries in this category, including Brazil, Malaysia, Mexico, Russia, South Korea and, most importantly, the two Asian giants, China and India. While some fractions of their populations still essentially live in the so-called Third World, significant numbers use IT-based infrastructures. These nations have around a million mobile phone and Internet users, which means 10% penetration for the smaller countries. The larger countries are all developing significant indigenous populations of scientific and engineering personnel and are pursuing greater international roles, for example in electronic commerce. All increasingly depend on IT-based infrastructures, notably in the transport, communications and finance sectors.

The rest of the world makes up a third category of more than 130 countries. About 50 of these comprise what the UN classifies as Least Developed Countries (that is, countries with the lowest per capita economic and infrastructure indicators). It is remarkable that almost all of these countries have some non-trivial connectivity to major international IT-based infrastructures. As of early 2000, over 220 more-or-less sovereign entities (for example, Hong Kong, which still has its own Top Level Domain name) were connected to the Internet, and most were connected to other network-based infrastructures, notably for banking and civil aviation.

Countries in the second and third categories will have an increasingly large stake in the international IT-based infrastructures in general, and in the Internet in particular. This is a result of three important factors. First, the great majority of their populations are under 30 years of age. Second, the low cost of access, at least compared with that of the other technology-based infrastructures such as transport, makes it possible for great numbers of formerly 'excluded' people to have global connectivity. Finally, most governments are either encouraging such connectivity, or at least no longer opposing it as they once did. Regional projections for Internet-using populations estimate that the Asia-Pacific will have more users by 2005 than the US, Canada and Western Europe combined.[3]

A fourth category consists of the managers, owners and opera-

tors of several important specialised transnational infrastructures that
have limited or controlled access. These infrastructures include several transport, energy, banking and finance networks. They are not
owned by any single government and are often partially privately
owned or operated. They may be partly governed by international
bodies, usually with the participation of specialised national government bodies in each of the countries that use them. Each specialised
transnational infrastructure has a readily identifiable set of operators
with a tradition of working together. These infrastructures may be
more effectively protected by their operators and primary international constituents, with lesser direct roles for national governments,
than may be the case for more general and publicly accessible infrastructures.

Applying the Strategic Framework generically

A brief and necessarily more speculative 'ensemble analysis' of the
advanced countries in the first category suggests that all of them will
fall into Cases II or IV. The technological and other demands of trying
to thwart attacks or limit damage, as defined in Chapter 3, are such
that no country can realistically claim to be confident of such capabilities at present. Therefore, Cases I and III define forms of defensive
strategies and capabilities that can at best be aspired to. Most of the
countries in this category should be able to build capabilities for
thwarting attacks to prevent damage so that their governments could
work on a Case II basis, if they wanted to. Most would not consider a
severe blow to their economy or security within the next five years to
be very likely, and hence would not make rapid defensive preparations a priority, although certain countries, such as Israel, might well
do so. More would have their remaining profiles closer to that of the
UK rather than the US because of the ways their infrastructures are
owned and operated, and would have a greater tolerance for, and perhaps expectation of, government regulation. At least a quarter of
these countries are thought to be looking into some form of offensive
information warfare. Few have the indigenous capabilities of either
the UK or the US, although most have some such capability.

All of the emerging players in the second category of nations
would also fall into Cases II or IV, but with a larger fraction in Case
IV than was true of the first category. Many of these countries have
the ability to pursue damage prevention for their relatively less exten-

sive infrastructure dependencies, and could well do so as a result of an assessment of the need for national critical infrastructure protection. Several might also see a need to be prepared within the next five years. Most of these latter countries are likely to be particularly close to the US (for example, Saudi Arabia) or in some way hostile to the US (for example, China). There may be at least a dozen countries in this category looking into options for offensive information warfare. The majority of these countries have fairly sparse infrastructure markets, and there is more government ownership and regulation than in the first category of countries. In many, the private sector is too weak, and foreign investment not sufficient, to provide infrastructure to serve large poor populations. Almost all are giving serious attention to building infrastructure, and some are doing so rapidly, particularly in telecommunications. However, relatively few are believed to be giving serious attention to infrastructure protection.

The great majority of the countries in the third category are in Case IV. The cyber element in their critical infrastructures is limited. For many, electrical power is so unreliable that frequent outages are regarded as normal. This even applies to the infrastructures used by the military, but probably not to its top levels. This is changing, although not as extensively as for the first two categories of countries. The changes are most relevant to the small sections of the population – often well under 10% – that have the education and money to want and need connectivity to function at a higher level. The infrastructures that are showing more cyber elements are telecommunications, banking systems and international transport systems. Almost all is of foreign origin, and in many cases is still under foreign control of one form or another, and much of its use is to connect with foreign entities.

This access and connectivity makes each of these countries a potential platform for generating trouble that affects networked critical infrastructures elsewhere. There are examples, such as the Philippines, where this has been the case. This is somewhat similar to the Y2K concern, where more advanced countries were worried about 'pollution' spreading from less capable LDCs. Unfortunately, the governments of the great majority of these LDCs have given infrastructure protection little or no thought, lack the necessary technical capability and are not able to deal with the problem in substantive ways.

Few of these countries would probably see the need to prepare for a severe blow to their economy or security in the next five years. The exceptions are mostly those who perceive a threat from the US, and these are probably the same countries that are looking into offensive information warfare. With few exceptions, there is little dependency on these infrastructures. Infrastructure markets are sparse and government ownership or regulation is common, although embryonic private participation, mostly in Internet and cellular phone provision, is becoming more common in many countries.

For the LDC governments, as the benefits of an increasingly global economy are acquired, so new risks emerge. They are not able to deal with these risks, principally because resources are limited. However, they can learn how to defend themselves. It is not very expensive, and help should be given by the more advanced countries and international organisations. Such action is a sound step in their own defence.

For the governments of the more advanced countries, a large part of the risk may reside outside their territories in countries whose governments are not capable of contributing much to their own, not to mention the common, defence. They need assistance. Possible models may be along the lines of the US–led international support to deal with the Y2K problem. This stimulated international interest and remedial action successfully in the short term. Another approach is to set up an international agreement with attendant capability-building organisations; a good example is the role of the International Civil Aviation Organisation (ICAO) in developing the civil aviation infrastructure.[4]

The fourth and last category, the managers and owners/operators of transnational infrastructures, could also benefit from assessments along the lines of the framework presented here. Their more narrowly defined scopes of coverage (a single networked infrastructure with more restricted access) could permit more focused efforts and successes. In particular, they may be better able to pursue attack prevention and especially damage limitation. They are in greater control of the technology of the systems they own and operate, and so are in a better position to develop and implement new technology. They are also less constrained by investigative efforts (such as privacy matters in data collection) than national governments that are concerned with infrastructures that support broad public access. Most of these are currently Case II entities, but might aspire to Case I or III more readily than a national government concerned with a broader spectrum of critical infrastructures. Perhaps the most pointed examples in this regard are civil aviation and banking and finance.[5]

The rest of the profiles for these entities, as defined by the framework, are also simple in comparison to those for national governments. In particular, they might all see a need to be prepared to deal with a cyber-attack within the next five years, and presumably none has offensive information-warfare ambitions. They operate in a relatively simple organisational domain and have years of experience working together internationally, sharing certain kinds of information, and developing and deploying technical and information standards.

Sweden as an example

A number of governments in the first category have already expressed concerns about infrastructure protection, and have taken measures to deal with the problem. A geographically dispersed sample includes Canada, Japan, Norway, Singapore and Sweden. A short, explicit application of the framework to Sweden will be illustrative.

Sweden clearly qualifies as a technically and economically advanced country with a range of modern infrastructures and connections to the rest of the world. Its population of about 10m people is far smaller than the UK's, but its land size is far larger. Over 2m people and a disproportionately large part of the infrastructure are concentrated within a 100-mile radius of Stockholm. The rest of the country is sparsely settled. Swedish policies have traditionally given considerable attention to national cohesion, and this includes the provision of extensive services to rural areas. As a result, Swedish towns and villages, despite difficult weather and terrain conditions, have some of the world's highest penetration rates for infrastructures such as electric power, telecommunications, the Internet and emergency services.

In 1996, the Swedish government established an advisory body now known as the Cabinet Working Group on Defensive Information Operations/Critical Infrastructure Protection (Cabinet WG). Under the leadership of the Ministry of Defence, it has wide interagency representation and participation, including the Cabinet Departments for Foreign Affairs, Justice and Treasury, the National Post and Telecommunications Agency and the Agency for Civil Emergency

Planning (OCB). The Cabinet WG and OCB provided most of the following information.[6]

The Swedish Parliament (the Riksdag) has identified 18 critical functions, several of which map directly onto IT-dependent infrastructures, including telecommunications, emergency services, transport, financial services and energy supply. Most of these have international connectivity. For example, Sweden is part of a regionally-connected electric power grid that extends into parts of the former Soviet Union.

Like the US, the Cabinet WG believes that Sweden should be prepared to deal with a serious cyber-attack on the national infrastructure within the next five years. As in the US and UK, there is little confidence that serious, expert and well-supported attacks can be prevented. The Swedes recognise that their ability to unilaterally deter attacks or punish attackers is limited. The government believes that it and its constituents can do much more to thwart or deflect attacks. This is seen as technically feasible, and the country has, or can develop or acquire, the necessary technology. The Swedes do not believe that limiting damage is feasible, but think the technology to achieve this option should be pursued in the longer term. Thus, Sweden emerges as a Case II country with near-term concerns. Emphasis should be placed on terminal defence, including cooperative terminal defence, and emergency management and reconstitution.

There is a substantial amount of mixed ownership of Sweden's critical infrastructures. For example, Svenska Kraftnat is a state-owned business with system-operator authority for the national electricity grid. Swedish demographics and policies are such that there is comparatively less foreign presence in ownership or operation than is the case for most countries in the first category, including the US and the UK.

A great deal of government regulation has been accepted. Furthermore, Sweden has a Total Defence concept for widespread national involvement in and concern for homeland defence and emergency services. There is an expectation that all will participate as necessary. The Riksdag has assigned responsibility for civil defence and emergency preparedness to a specific government agency or board for each of the 18 critical functions. Each of these deals with the appropriate parts of the private sector.

The Swedish market structure is sparse in comparison with

those of the US and the UK. Sweden is relatively self-sufficient, but too small to support many suppliers and highly differentiated market segments domestically. It is best known internationally for its competitive industrial strength in areas such as transport, telecommunications and defence. This is the result of the extraordinary ability of a small country to create and support some very large firms, and the organisations needed for this.

For the most part, current infrastructure protection activities in Sweden are consistent with this assessment. The Cabinet WG, in collaboration with a wide range of other government agencies, is developing a comprehensive national plan, and the subject is receiving attention at the ministry and parliamentary levels.

The prospective coordinating agency will be the OCB. The OCB has a long history of national assessments, planning and facilitating the agencies engaged in operations over a broad range of infrastructure domains, including electric power, telecommunications and transport. It has put considerable effort into making companies and government agencies aware of the vulnerabilities of information systems.

The OCB has undertaken security analyses of almost 500 IT systems at the national and local government levels and in industry. In 1998, the OCB introduced the FA22 provisions and guidelines for information systems. All of the approximately 400 Swedish national and regional preparedness agencies must comply with FA22. As has been the case in all other countries that have made such attempts, the analyses of these important systems revealed a great many deficiencies in access authorisation, failure planning, management and recovery procedures.

The Cabinet WG has proposed a number of specific approaches and responsibilities for information assurance.[7] Among these are the extensive use of penetration teams to test systems and the creation of an effective government Computer Emergency Response Team (CERT). Particular attention is being given to information collection, sharing and intelligence. Authorisation is being pursued with the Riksdag and other government agencies.

The Cabinet WG and OCB are confident that they can work with public and private owners and operators. There is a long history to support this view. The Swedes have built considerable physical redundancy into their electric power, telecommunications and transport systems as a matter of civil-defence policy. There are also extensive military and civil traditions in emergency and recovery services. The importance of the reconstitution and recovery of important infrastructures is probably more broadly established in Sweden than in either the UK or the US.

Sweden recognises that many of its vulnerabilities and threats arise from extensive international connectivity. The Swedes also recognise that they cannot effectively prevent attacks entirely on their own, and feel that forms of international cooperation will be necessary if much is to be done in this regard. They have a long and active history of international participation and aid.

Conclusion

The introduction of information technology into the operation of infrastructures has opened them up to the danger of cyber-attack, and their natural interdependencies multiply the potential risk to the countries that depend upon them. The number of attacks on infrastructures is increasing, as is the severity of their impact. The exploitation of these vulnerabilities can result in new strategic threats to national security.

The potential for building viable commercial and governmental structures on state-of-the-art public information infrastructure is open to question unless the vulnerability concerns considered in this paper are more fully addressed. Current information systems and practices leave sensitive personal, commercial and government information and facilities open to theft, modification or denial. Unless better approaches to protection are implemented and their effectiveness demonstrated, extending information technology to new domains should be of concern.

Reducing infrastructure vulnerability to cyber-attack is an inherently global issue that will require global responses. Countries share in the operation and the benefits of global infrastructures. Attackers can be located anywhere and the cost of entry into this domain of warfare is widely affordable, in terms of the capital and human resources required. International cooperation will be needed if the technical skills and organisational structures necessary to combat it are to be mobilised.

Currently, this problem is being addressed by a handful of highly-industrialised countries, including the US, the UK and Sweden. Since major growth in the application of information technology is yet to appear in the rest of the world, there is ample opportunity to take cooperative action to reduce what could become a worldwide problem.

Nations will be best served by seeking to strengthen the defence of their information-dependent infrastructures through individual and collective action. Individual action by owners and operators of infrastructure systems will, depending on circumstances, be based on either market-driven decisions or central government regulation. Collective action to share threat and vulnerability information and to deter attackers through effective detection and prosecution will rely on both voluntary agreements among system operators and users, and international agreements.

Action to reduce the threats discussed here will be most effective if there is a consensus on the nature of the threat and the need for remedial action. In particular, it will be important to balance priorities for nearer- and longer-term approaches if an adequate level of global protection is to be achieved. To this end, sharing data on current attacks on information systems is important in facilitating rational decision-making.

A cost-effective approach would seek to evolve system architectures in ways that will reduce their vulnerability. If this can be done, costly post-deployment remedies will be minimised. In particular, the rate of development of telecommunications, information and other IT-based infrastructures in a large number of the countries in the second and third categories is extremely rapid. But these countries will be hard-pressed to do much on their own, which means that the countries in the first category will have to provide leadership and assistance.

If governments are to take effective action against the growing vulnerability of infrastructures, they will need to formulate and implement coherent long-term strategies, both individually and collectively. The strategic framework presented here provides guidance for constructing and implementing such strategies. When applied to the US, the UK and Sweden, the framework seems to address the first-order set of issues facing national decision-makers.

In applying the strategic framework to the US and the UK, both their similarities and differences are made explicit. The US policy is to be prepared for a possible infrastructure attack sooner than is the case in the UK. This, according to the framework, should mean that the US is putting greater emphasis on nearer-term measures, but these are

difficult to implement because neither private-sector system operators nor the managers of government funding appear willing to allo-
cate sufficient resources. Instead, US measures appear better suited to
a longer-term approach that involves R&D, training security professionals and encouraging the sharing of information related to vulnerability and threat assessments.

The UK policy is to plan for a later date of readiness and thereby, according to the framework, to assess the threats more fully and
to build consensus for action before making major commitments.
Thus, the focus here is on establishing the necessary legal framework,
building the intra-government mechanisms for the control of cyber-
crime and terrorism, setting technical standards for system and network security and harmonising its actions with European Union
regulatory initiatives. However, other longer-term opportunities for
progress, such as R&D and improving the preparation of the engineers who will design and operate more secure and robust infrastructure systems, do not appear to be recognised to the same degree.

An unanswered question is the feasibility of near real-time
monitoring of systems to enable the operation of adaptive defence
measures and damage limitation – the information-system analogues
of the military doctrines of situation awareness and battle management. Such approaches present a number of technical difficulties and
raise issues of privacy and the possible compromise of national
sovereignty.

A fundamental issue presented by the introduction of information technology is the degree to which it is an enabler of efficient and
effective functionality while still able to provide sufficient protection
to run stable and reliable systems. Alternatively, the technology's
inevitable complexity is exploited by attackers, leading to the need for
international agreements that have as their goal deterrence, arms control and non-proliferation. While this dichotomy between construc-
tive and destructive uses is common to all technologies, the rapid
spread of information technology makes resolving this issue particularly urgent. While advanced technology usually remains in the
hands of a few specialists who can be trained and licensed in its use,
information technology lends itself to wide misuse through malevolence, carelessness and irresponsibility. This argues for urgent strategic planning on a national scale before passing *a* point of no return, if
this has not already occurred.

Notes

Acknowledgements

The authors wish to thank their colleagues David Elliott, Edward Feigenbaum and John Woods at the Stanford University Center for International Security and Cooperation for their careful reading of the manuscript and for their thoughtful comments, and research assistants Cynthia Patterson and Andrea Littman at the Sam Nunn School of International Affairs at Georgia Institute of Technology for their invaluable efforts.

Chapter 1

1 A number of countries have addressed this concern. For example, in the US the Clinton administration's 'White Paper on Critical Infrastructure Protection: Presidential Decision Directive 63' (22 May 1998) notes: 'As a result of advances in information technology and the necessity of improving efficiency ¼ [of the nation's critical] infrastructures have become increasingly automated and interlinked. These same advances have created new vulnerabilities to ¼ physical and cyber attacks'. An article written by Will Knight, 'Hackers Become Terrorists under UK Law', 20 February 2001, quotes UK Home Secretary Jack Straw as saying: '[Terrorists] are no respecters of borders and are continuously developing new approaches and techniques. With the implementation of the Terrorism Act 2000, the UK is making a very firm statement of our intent to combat terrorism.' The Act makes the 'deliberate interference with electronic systems' an offence. The government has broadened the definition of terrorism to include computer-related activity because it is concerned that militant groups are increasingly turning to computer hacking techniques. The home secretary signalled that he intends to clamp down on those exploiting computers and the Internet to perpetrate terrorist

activity. (The article is available at www.zdnet.com.au). Lars Nicander, secretary to the Swedish Cabinet Working Group on IO-D/CIP, notes in a paper entitled 'Information Operations - A Swedish View' that: 'the threat against the information society has become increasingly important at the same time as systems and functions important to the society are becoming more dependent on information technology. The question of society's vulnerability in this respect has a strong bearing on security policy'. Canadian Prime Minister Jean Chrétien has stated: 'The protection of Canada's critical infrastructure from the risks of failure or disruption is essential to assuring the health, safety, security and economic well-being of Canadians'. Office of the Prime Minister, press release, 5 February 2001. In Japan, the Ministry of International Trade and Industry (MITI) has established a committee chaired by Professor Tomio Umeda of Chiba Institute of Technology to study protective measures against cyber-terrorism. Based on case studies, the committee presented a set of urgently-required protection measures. See www.meti.go.jp/english/report/data/g316001e.html. At a conference at Stanford University, CA, on 6-7 December 1999, Raisuka Miyawaki noted that 'those who are preparing for cyber-crime and cyber-terrorism in the world ... see Japan's infrastructure lifelines as a global pressure point. A cyber attack on Japan's vulnerable financial, economic, transportation and defence networks would have substantial effects outside Japan. And such an attack could be sent from anywhere in the world'. Other countries, among them Australia and Israel, have also recognised the need to address these concerns.

2 UK infrastructures were studied by Ernst & Young for the Cabinet Office, as part of the Y2K effort. The study is on the Cabinet Office website at www.citu.gov.uk/2000/ey_study/ey_menu.htm.

3 The times given are from when the site was available to legitimate users less than 5% of the time, to when the site was available at least 80% of the time.

4 These numbers are from the New York Times, 10 February 2000. Further statistical information can be found in a Keynote Systems press release of 12 February 2000 at www.keynote.com/press/html/00feb12.html.

5 Apart from the details, the major lesson from these distributed denial of service attacks is that any site can be put out of action in this way. Not only are there direct losses to the businesses so attacked, but such attacks put in question the feasibility of a stable e-commerce environment. The perpetrators of such attacks are extremely difficult to identify. These attacks were launched with a software tool available on the Web that requires little technical ability to use. One 15-year-old Canadian was charged with two counts of criminal mischief for

the attack against CNN (*New York Times*, 20 April 2000), confirming the ease with which such attacks can be launched.

6 Richard Power, 'How To Quantify Financial Losses from Infosec Breaches', Computer Security Institute, *Alert: The Newsletter for Information Protection Professionals*, October 1999. In the case of these attacks, the sites themselves minimised the damage. CNN reported no loss of advertising revenue, but market-research firms estimated the total loss from all the attacks to be the number used here. They also suggest that either the firms lack a reliable way of establishing what their losses are, making risk management difficult, or they do not want to alarm their investors (*New York Times*, 20 April 2000). In addition to the losses to the businesses attacked, their Internet Service Provider (ISP) and the ISP's other customers also suffer inconvenience and losses due to network congestion. US Deputy Attorney-General Eric Holder suggested that the attacks had a negative impact on the stock market on 9 February (ibid., 11 February 2000). Others questioned whether the attack had an impact on Buy.com's IPO the day of the attack, but the conclusions on this point varied (ibid., 9 February 2000).

7 Andrew Norfolk, Simon de Bruxelles and Russell Jenkins 'Motorists Hit as Protest Spreads Across Country', *The Times* 11 September 2000, www. times-archive.co.uk; Peter Hetherington, Patrick Wintour and Charlotte Denny, 'Panic as Oil Blockade Bites', *The Guardian*, www.guardian.co.uk.

8 The same can be said of the IRA plan to attack six power stations supplying London in 1997. Estimates at the time indicated that, had the attack succeeded, electrical supplies would have been severely affected for several months with the consequent interdependency effects suggested in Table 1. See 'IRA "Planned To Black Out London"', *The Telegraph*, 12 April 1997, www.telegraph.co.uk.

9 Angelique Chrisafis, 'Schools Forced To Close and Hospitals Cancel Ops', *The Guardian* 16 September 2000, www.guardianunlimited.co.uk.

10 Conal Urquhart, Russell Jenkins, Gillian Harris and Paul Wilkinson, 'Filling Stations Will Remain Dry for Days', *The Times* 15 September 2000, www. times-archive.co.uk.

11 'Fuel Crisis: The Cost to Business', BBC News, news.bbc.co.uk.

12 The Carnegie Mellon Software Engineering Institute CERT Coordination Center recorded 21,756 attacks in the US alone in 2000. See www.cert.org/stats/cert_stats.html. The comparable number of attacks in 1995 was 2,412. In 1999, 22,144 attacks were detected on Defense Department systems. Walter Pincus, 'Hits on Pentagon Computers Are Up 10% in 2000', *Washington Post*, 9 December 2000. See also 'Information Security Computer Attacks at Department of Defense Pose Increasing Risks',

GAO/AIMD-96-84, 22 May 1996; 'Information /Security Opportunities for Improved OMB Oversight of Agency Practices', GAO/AIMD-96-110, 24 September 1996. The data for these attacks show that 67% were successful, of which only 4% were detected, and only 27% of these were reported. Thus, reports of successful attacks possibly represent only 1% of the total. In contrast, attacks on commercial systems studied by Richard Power suggest higher reporting rates. For system penetration from the outside, the reporting rate was 42%. See 'CSI/FBI Computer Crime and Security Survey', Computer Security Institute, *Computer Security Issues & Trends*, vol. 3, no. 1, Winter 2000

[13] Although in one attack, a Swedish hacker shut down some emergency phone systems in Florida. Associated Press, 4 March 1997.

[14] Raymond Parks et al., 'Modeling Behaviour of the Cyber-Terrorist', CRISP-CISAC-Hoover National Security Forum, Stanford University, Stanford, CA, 6-7 December 1999.

[15] The complexity of software, in particular commercial off-the-shelf software that is widely used in infrastructure systems, results in numerous entry points for cyber-attacks. For example, the CERT Coordination Center was notified of 744 security flaws in widely-used commercial software in 2000, up from 171 in 1995. See www.cert.org/stats/cert_stats.ht ml. These flaws are well-known

to attackers because information about them is published to help those responsible for defending information systems. But attackers are frequently faster at exploiting flaws than defenders are in patching them up.

Chapter 2

[1] Stephen J. Lukasik, 'Public and Private Roles in the Protection of Critical Information-Dependent Infrastructure', Center for International Security and Cooperation, Stanford University, May 1997.

[2] An example of such an international legal structure can be found in Abraham D. Sofaer et al., 'A Proposal for an International Convention on Cyber Crime and Terrorism', Center for International Security and Cooperation, Stanford University, CA, August 2000.

Chapter 3

[1] Continuing attacks on a system, such as in Figure 2, offer the possibility of responding in near real-time. This will be the case when the interval over which the attacks occur is sufficiently long for the defender to recognise the attacker and to install software 'alarms' to signal the attacker's presence. An example of this is described by Clifford Stoll in *The Cuckoo's Egg: Tracking a Spy Through the Maze of Computer Espionage* (New York: Doubleday, 1989). But being aware of this possibility, attackers attempt to vary their approach to avoid being recognised.

2 Stephen J. Lukasik, 'Systems, Systems of Systems, and the Education of Engineers', *Artificial Intelligence for Engineering Design, Analysis, and Manufacturing*, vol. 12, 1998, pp. 55–60.

3 Stephen J. Lukasik and Michael Erlinger, 'Educating Designers of Complex Systems: Information Networks as a Testbed', *International Journal of Engineering Education*, vol. 17, April 2001, pp. 460–67.

Chapter 4

1 Stephen J. Lukasik, 'Protecting the Global Information Commons', *Telecommunications Policy*, Delft, Netherlands, vol. 24, 2000, pp. 519–31.

Chapter 5

1 Executive Order 13010, 15 July 1996. This established the President's Commission on Critical Infrastructure Protection; the Executive Order was amended on 13 November 1996.

2 Information regarding infrastructure performance can be found through the respective regulatory bodies: see the Federal Energy Regulatory Commission (www.ferc.fed.us); US Nuclear Regulatory Commission (www.nrc.gov/nrc.html); North American Electric Reliability Council (www.nerc.com); Federal Communications Commission (www.fcc.gov/indstats.html); Network Reliability and Interoperability Council (www.nric.org); Federal Trade Commission (www.ftc.gov); US Securities and Exchange Commission (www.sec.gov). For information regarding state regulatory commissions, see the National Association of Regulatory Utility Commissioners (www.naruc.org/stateweb.htm).

3 Stephen J. Lukasik, 'Current and Future Technical Capabilities', Chapter 2 in Abraham Sofaer and Seymour Goodman, *Cyber Crime and Security: The Transnational Dimension* (Stanford, CA: Hoover Institution Press, 2001).

4 'Critical Foundations: Protecting America's Infrastructures', The Report of the President's Commission on Critical Infrastructure Protection, October 1997.

5 Richard Power, 'CSI/FBI Computer Crime and Security Survey', Computer Security Institute, *Computer Security Issues & Trends*, vol. 6, Spring 2000. See www.gocsi.com.

6 The Clinton Administration's Policy on Critical Infrastructure Protection: Presidential Decision Directive 63, 22 May 1998.

7 'A National Security Strategy for a New Century', The White House, December 1999.

8 Gigabit network research community refers to new developments by the research community in higher speed networks. See www.caida.org. CAIDA, the Cooperative Association for Internet Data Analysis, is located at the University of California San Diego Supercomputer Center. See also the work of the co-located National Laboratory for Applied Network Research at www.nlanr.net.

9 Robert Richardson, 'Enterprise Anti-Virus Software', *Network Magazine*, 1 February 2000; Kim Zetter, 'Viruses', *PC World*, vol. 18, December 2000, p. 191.

10 While automated intrusion detection is the subject of ongoing R&D and the development of Internet protocols to support such a capability under the auspices of the Internet Engineering Task Force, it is not currently available. See www.ietf.org.

11 The Federal Trade Commission plays a regulatory role in the protection of online personal information. See www.ftc.gov/privacy/index.html. The Gramm-Leach-Billey Act (Public Law 106-102, Title V, Privacy) establishes restrictions on the disclosure of personal financial information and its sharing among affiliates of financial institutions.

12 In the Secretary of Defense Annual Report to the President and the Congress for 1998, Information Operations (IO) are defined as: 'actions taken across the entire conflict spectrum to affect adversary information and information systems while protecting one's own information and information systems. Information warfare is conducted during crisis or conflict to achieve specific objectives over an adversary. Information assurance protects and defends information and information systems by ensuring their availability, integrity, authenticity, and confidentiality'. See www.dtic.mil/execsec/adr98/chap8.html. The Annual Report for 2000 expands consider-

ably on what started as Command, Control and Communication into what is now called Information Superiority. The report explains: 'The information age provides an opportunity to move from an approach to war preoccupied with uncertainty and damage control to one that leverages information to create competitive advantage. The United States currently enjoys a superior information position over potential adversaries by virtue of its ability to collect, process and distribute relevant and accurate information in a timely manner *while denying this capability to adversaries* (emphasis added).' See www.dtic.mil/execsec/adr2000/chap8.html. The report lists a number of goals of information superiority, one of which is to implement programmes in critical infrastructure protection, i.e., 'the protection of the critical assets and infrastructures DoD [Department of Defense] relies upon to accomplish its mission'. It also notes that the Department 'must work with allies and coalition partners to protect information since, in an interconnected world, this translates into the ability to protect DoD's information and critical infrastructure'. The 2001 report says: 'Information operations support the objectives of the National Security Strategy by enhancing information superiority and influencing foreign perceptions ... The Department's emerging concept for IO will be the basis for aligning strategy and policy across DoD. When approved, the strategic concept will guide and integrate IO policy, organisation, and implementation in the research, development, and acquisition of IO capabilities.' See www.dtic.mil/execsec/adr2001/chap8.html.

[13] In a press briefing on 6 July 2000, Secretary of Defense William S. Cohen pointed out: 'We have a very active program to try and protect and deter any terrorist actions taking place ... We are focusing on that as one of the most serious threats we'll have to contend with. Cyber terrorism, weapons of mass destruction. But cyber terrorism can cause catastrophic harm as well. So we are spending a good deal of our resources building up our capacity to defend our critical infrastructure to protect against not only the Love Bug type of attacks, but dedicated professionals from various countries who have teams of professionals who are looking for ways in which they can attack the critical infrastructures of the United States, shutting down air traffic control, the energy systems we have, the distribution of energy, our financial systems, and many other types of critical infrastructure that we have.' See www.defenselink.mil/news/Jul2000/t07072000_t0706sd.html.

[14] Robert Parry, 22 March 2001, www.consortium-news/1999/050499a.html.

[15] To this end a US/UK team of researchers, working under the auspices of the IISS, met a representative group of UK policy-makers, infrastructure service providers, and analysts in July–October 2000. Through such mechanisms as workshops, meetings and reviews of available literature, the framework of Chapter 4 was tested for its applicability.

[16] See wood.ccta.gov.uk/homeoffice, 6 March 2001.

[17] BBC News, 15 September 2000, news.bbc.co.uk.

[18] www.niscc.gov.uk/aboutniscc/nisccinfo.htm.

[19] Among the many commercial security products available worldwide are those provided by Cisco (www.cisco.com); Internet Security Systems (www.iss.net); Network Associates (www.nai.com); and Aladdin (www.aladdin.com).

[20] Official threat assessments do not specify a time period of concern. Informal discussions with policy-makers focused on the need to address credible worst-case threats, the implication being that some discussions of high-level threats were not. In other discussions, infrastructure was noted as being 'self-healing'. The official position as stated by Mike O'Brien, Home Office minister, is that: 'IT systems across Government and business are becoming increasingly interconnected and important to our everyday lives. This opens up unprecedented benefits, but also creates new vulnerabilities in our IT systems that could be exploited. In the future it is likely that the incidence and severity of electronic attacks will increase.

Therefore sensible precautions must be taken to ensure IT systems are robust and proportionate protective security measures are in place'. This suggests that the current degree of connectivity is not yet a cause for undue alarm. It was also noted in private discussions that IT and the construction of complex information systems is changing so rapidly that current threat assessments might have to be revised. While the threat at the nation-state level appears to be low, it was noted that public expectations regarding the security of information were increasing. In an open letter to Critical National Infrastructure managers, 2 December 1999, it was stated that: 'the threat of an orchestrated attack aimed at the infrastructure is currently assessed as low, but it could grow quickly without warning'. At the 27 September 2000 inauguration of the Security Forum, George Normand, director of the NISCC, said the threat is 'very high for some systems, low for the infrastructure as a whole, but that it could rise fast'.

21 Input packet traffic refers to data packets that enter a computer system from the outside.

22 Jack Straw, Home Office, 28 June 2000, www.parliament.the-stationery-office.co.uk.

23 At the 6 March 2001 Information Assurance Conference, it was noted that more emphasis is being placed on raising the awareness of industry. A brochure, prepared by the IAAC and being circulated by the Institute of Directors, urges adoption of BS 7799 as a baseline standard. See www.iaac.ac.uk.

24 These are currently being developed and deployed for key national systems, such as those used for defence. The use of real-time monitoring is crucial as defence connectivity with the Internet, in the main for e-commerce reasons, increases. Similarly, some banks use real-time monitoring systems. But the degree to which they have a 'battle management' capability and the organisations employing them have developed operational doctrines for real-time response is unknown.

25 While government policy backs privatisation, it is likely that most functions that can be privatised have been.

26 For example, OFTEL (the regulator for the UK telecommunications industry) sees a role in digital communications, but European legislation only reflects analogue communication.

27 See www.ofgas.gov.uk/public/domelec.htm; and www.oftel.gov.uk/ind_info/licensing/oftlic_c.htm.

Chapter 6

1 'National Plan for Information Systems Protection, Version 1.0', The White House, Washington DC, December 2000.

2 'Report of the President of the United States on the States of Federal Critical Infrastructure Protection Activities', The White House, January 2001. See http://www.ciao.gov/CIAO_Document_Library/CIP_2001_CongR

ept.pdf.

3 National Security Presidential Directive-1, Organisation of the National Security Council System, 13 February 2001. See www.fas.org/irp/offdocs/nspd/nspd-1.htm. See also Dan Verton, 'Bush Advisor Urges Increased Cybercrime Cooperation', www.infoworld.com.

4 George W. Bush, 'Critical Infrastructure Protection in the Information Age', The White House, Washington DC. Executive Order 13231, 16 October 2001.

5 'The National Strategy to Secure Cyberspace,' The White House, Washington, DC.

6 See www.pcis.org

7 The NSTAC Network Group has examined the impact of the Internet in a report published in July 1999, 'Internet Report: An Examination of the NS/EP Implications of Internet Technologies'.

8 'Critical Infrastructure Protection: Who's in Charge?', statement by John S. Tritac, director of the Critical Infrastructure Assurance Office, before the Senate Committee on Governmental Affairs, 4 October 2001. See www.ogc.gov/ogc/legreg/testimon/107f/tritac1004.htm.

9 See www.nipc.gov.

10 Wade Roush, 'Networking the Infrastructure', *Technology Review*, December 2001, pp. 39–41.

11 'Wiretapping System Works on Internet, Review Finds', *New York Times*, 24 November 2000; 'ACLU Urges Congress to Put a Leash on "Carnivore" and Other Government Snoopware

Programs', 12 July 2000, www.aclu.org/news/2000/n0712 00b.html; 'I-Spy: Critics Blast Cyber Snooping Device', 13 July 2000, usnews.about.com/newsissues/usnews/library/weekly/aa 071300a.htm; Nicky Hager, 'Exposing the Global Surveillance System', www.dis.org/erehwon/echelon.html.

12 The lack of central management for privately-owned infrastructure makes the collection of such metrics difficult to organise. Of possible interest is the Government Performance and Results Act of 1993, which provides for the establishment of strategic planning and performance measurements in federal programmes, such as those supporting R&D in infrastructure security. Regulatory initiatives could also provide opportunities to establish system-wide performance metrics.

13 See the Cabinet Office website, www.cabinet-office.gov.uk; and www.ukonline.gov.uk.

14 Cabinet Office press release, 18 April 2000; Margaret Beckett, Leader of the House, announced that Y2K infrastructure work will be taken forward as a weapon in the fight to combat cyber-crime.

15 Jack Straw, Home Secretary. See www.niscc.gov.uk.

16 e-government bulletin, 30 August 2000, www.iib.com/news.html.

17 www.cert.dfn.de/eng/csir/europe/fsig-93.html#ABS46.

18 www.janes.com/security/law_enforcement/market_reviews/asst/asst_03.shtml, August 1999. Note that this is in conflict

with the 1996 statistics in
www.brunel.ac.uk/~andrew/revi
ewsinformation-security-
colloq.html, IEEE colloquium,
27 June 1996.

[19] www.ncis.co.uk/press/
16_99.html.

[20] 'Trawler's Empty Net', *The
Guardian*, 24 June 1999,
www.guardianunlimited.co.uk.
On 13 November 2000, the Home
Secretary announced that an extra
£25m was being made available
to fight computer crime.

[21] These include: the Association of
British Insurers, the British
Computer Society, British
Telecommunications plc, the
Business Continuity Institute, the
Department of Trade and Industry
(DTI Information Security Policy
Group), Det Norske Veritas Quality
Assurance, HMG Protective
Security authority, HSBC, Indicii
Salus, the Institute of Chartered
Accountants in England and Wales,
the Institute of Internal Auditors,
KPMG plc, L3 Network Security,
Lloyds TSB, Logica UK, Marks and
Spencer plc, the Nationwide
Building Society, PCSL, Racal
Network Services, RKP Associates,
Shell International Petroleum Co
Ltd, Unilever plc, Whitbread plc
and XiSEC Consultants Ltd/AEXIS
Consultants.

[22] See www.dti.gov.uk/PROTECT/
confidential/appenda.htm; and
www.bsi.org.uk.

[23] BS 7799 has also become an ISO
standard, ISO 17799.

[24] ww.cesg.gov.uk.

[25] www.hmso.gov.uk/acts/
acts1997/1997004.htm.

[26] See www.parliament.the-sta-

tionery-office.co.uk; and
www.fei.org.uk, 8 May 2000.

[27] www.parliament.the-stationery-
office.co.uk/pa/1d199900/1dbills
/061/en/00061x—.htm.

[28] 'Information Security Breaches
2000', www.dti.gov.uk.

[29] R&D groups exist at Cambridge
University (www.cl.cam.ac.uk/
users/rja14/); Newcastle
University (www.cs.ncl.ac.uk/
people/brian.randell); Salford
University (www.salford.ac.uk/
iti/dwc/chadwick.html); Royal
Holloway College (isg.rhbnc.
ac.uk/ Fred_Piper.htm);
University College London
(www-mice.cs.ucl.ac.uk/multi-
media/); and the London School
of Economics (www.csrc.lse.
ac.uk).

[30] www.dera.gov.uk.

[31] www.ja.net./topology//SJIII-
0300.gif, www.ja.net/topology/
external.html and www.super-
janet4.net /backbone_procure-
ment/index.html.

[32] Prime Minister Tony Blair,
Cabinet Office press release on
the appointment of Andrew
Pinder as e-Envoy, 31 January
2001. See www.cabinet-
office.gov.uk/2001/news/010131
_envoypinder.htm.

Chapter 7

[1] Internet Society (ISOC) Forum,
vol. 7, March 2001.

[2] For studies of the development
and absorption of the Internet,
see Peter Wolcott and Seymour E.
Goodman, 'The Internet in
Turkey and Pakistan: A
Comparative Analysis', Center for
International Security and

Cooperation, Stanford University, December 2000; S. E. Goodman, et al., 'The Global Diffusion of the Internet: An Initial Inductive Study', The MOSAIC Group, SAIC Center for Information Strategy and Policy, March 1998. (available on CD-ROM); William Foster and Seymour E. Goodman, 'The Diffusion of the Internet in China' (Palo Alto: Center for International Studies and Cooperation, Stanford University, 2000); Peter Wolcott and Seymour Goodman, 'The Diffusion of the Internet in India' (Georgia Tech Information Security Center/Center for International Security and Cooperation, Stanford University, 2002)

3 Jeffrey Harrow, 'The Coming Internet and Wireless Explosion', www.etforecasts.com/pr/pr201.htm, visited 26 February 2001.

4 Abraham D. Sofaer and Seymour E. Goodman (eds), *The Transnational Dimensions of Cyber Crime and Terrorism* (Stanford, CA: Hoover Institution Press, 2001).

5 In the US, the financial services industry operates an ISAC, managed by Global Integrity, as called for in its National Plan. See www.fsisac.com/fsisac_overview.htm.

6 'Measures and Protection Against Information Warfare – A proposal for Division of Responsibilities, etc.', Report number 2 (unclassified) from the Cabinet Working Group on Defensive Information Warfare (IO-D/IA), 19 September 1998. 'CEP in Sweden', Beredskap, The Swedish Agency for Civil Emergency Planning, no. 3/99,

October 1999, pp. 27–33. E. Anders Eriksson and Malin Fylkner, 'IT-Related Threats in the Network Society: Suggestions for a Swedish Proactive Agenda,' FOA [Defence Research Establishment], Draft, December 1999; Lars Nicander, 'Information Operations – A Swedish View', National Office of IO/CIP Studies, Stockholm, Sweden, 25 September 2000; set of organisational and mission briefing charts, National Defence College, November 2000. Most of these and other documents may be found translated into English at www.fhs.mil.se/utb/operativa/opi/ikk_eng.htm. Lars Nicander is Secretary of the Cabinet WG. We are grateful to him for the time he spent meeting one of the authors and setting up meetings with many others in Stockholm, 20–22 February 2001.

7 See in particular the ten recommendations given in 'Measures and Protection Against Information Warfare – A proposal for Division of Responsibilities, etc.', Report number 2 (unclassified) from the Cabinet Working Group on Defensive Information Warfare (IO-D/IA), 19 September 1998.

About the author

Stephen Lukasik is a physicist whose work has involved developing advanced technologies in both the public and private sectors. As Director of the US Department of Defense Advanced Research Projects Agency, he was an early participant in the development of the information network technologies.

Seymour Goodman is Professor of International Affairs and Computing at the Sam Nunn School of International Affairs and the College of Computing at the Georgia Institute of Technology and Co-Director of the Georgia Tech Information Security Center. His research has been in technology diffusion, national security, and related public policy issues.

David Longhurst is an electrical engineer and a senior member of the UK Ministry of Defence. He has been project manager of the NATO IV space programme and responsible for the formulation of the MoD information systems and communications strategy. He headed the MoD Year 2000 Millennium bug team and currently serves as Defence Information Advisor.

About **The International Institute for Strategic Studies**

The International Institute for Strategic Studies is an independent centre for research, information and debate on the problems of conflict, however caused, that have, or potentially have, an important military content. The Council and Staff of the Institute are international and its membership is drawn from over 90 countries. The Institute is independent and it alone decides what activities to conduct. It owes no allegiance to any government, any group of governments or any political or other organisation. The IISS stresses rigorous research with a forward-looking policy orientation and places particular emphasis on bringing new perspectives to the strategic debate.

The Institute's publications are designed to meet the needs of a wider audience than its own membership and are available on subscription, by mail order and in good bookshops.